Pam & Nicky Lintott

JELLY ROLL
QUILTS
IN A WEEKEND

15 Quick and Easy Quilt Patterns

sewandso

www.sewandso.co.uk

Contents

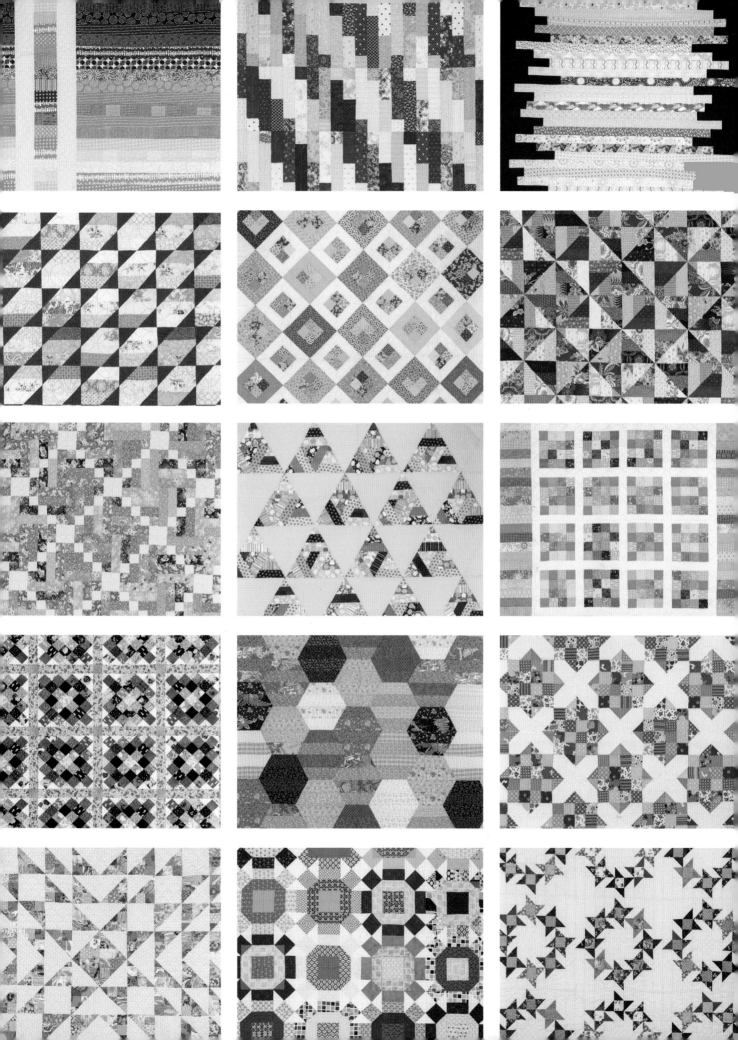

Introduction

There is so much you can do with a jelly roll that we never tire of them – forty strips of fabric wound up into such a delicious looking roll... gorgeous! It really is true that the most difficult thing about a jelly roll is unravelling it! Once you've done that, then you have before you forty different fabrics which will be the basis of your quilt. The colours all coordinate and you just have to decide on your quilt pattern. The quilts in this book use just one jelly roll. You may need some background fabric and possibly a border fabric for some quilts, but essentially your quilt top is made up of those forty fabrics. How amazing is that?

So, armed with your jelly roll, you just have to flick through the pages of this book to decide which quilt you are going to make this weekend. We have carefully selected designs that are quick and easy to put together and hopefully look far more complicated than they really are. We have timed the piecing of the quilts and each of them can be pieced in a weekend, and then all you have to do is the quilting and finishing off. Towards the end of the book we have designed a couple of quilts that may take a long weekend, but essentially over the space of a couple of days you can make any of these quilt tops. Sounds too good to be true? Just have a try!

We have placed the quilts in the book roughly in the time taken to make them, from the shortest to the longest. This is approximate and obviously there are going to be occasions when something takes a little longer than expected. However, none of the designs are difficult so just pick a quilt and off you go. Better still, meet up with a friend and have fun making two quilts!

Pam and Nicky

Getting Started

WHAT IS A JELLY ROLL?

Moda introduced jelly rolls to showcase new fabric ranges and a jelly roll is a roll of forty fabrics cut in 2½in wide strips across the width of the fabric. How inspirational to have one 2½in wide strip of each new fabric wrapped up so deliciously! Our thanks go to Moda for inspiring us and allowing us to use the name jelly roll in this book. All the quilt patterns here assume that fabric will be at least 42in wide. If you want to make any of the quilts in the book and don't have a jelly roll to use, then cut a 2½in wide strip from forty fabrics in your stash and you can follow all the instructions in just the same way to make a quilt.

IMPERIAL OR METRIC?

Jelly rolls from Moda are cut 2½in wide and at The Quilt Room we have continued to cut our strip bundles 2½in wide. When quilt making, it is impossible to mix metric and imperial measurements. It would be absurd to have a 2½in strip and tell you to cut it 6cm to make a square! It wouldn't be square and nothing would fit. This caused a dilemma when writing instructions for our quilts and a decision had to be made. All our instructions therefore are written in inches. To convert inches to centimetres, multiply the inch measurement by 2.54. For your convenience, any additional fabric you need is given in the You Will Need panel at the start of the quilt instructions, in both metric and imperial.

SEAM ALLOWANCE

We cannot stress enough the importance of maintaining an accurate *scant* ¼in seam allowance throughout. Please take the time to check your seam allowance with the test described in the General Techniques section.

QUILT SIZE

In this book we have shown what can be achieved with just one jelly roll (forty 2½in strips). We have sometimes added background fabric and borders but the basis of each quilt is just one jelly roll.

DIAGRAMS

Diagrams have been provided to assist you in making the quilts and these are normally beneath or beside the relevant stepped instruction. The direction in which fabric should be pressed is indicated by small arrows on the diagrams. The reverse side of the fabric is usually shown in a lighter colour than the right side.

WASHING NOTES

It is important that pre-cut strips are *not* washed before use. Save the washing until your quilt is complete and then make use of a colour catcher in the wash, or possibly dry clean the quilt.

BOARDWALK

This quilt is a delight to make and is so easy it just about makes itself. It's a perfect weekend project, and proof that designs do not have to be time-consuming and complicated to look great. We used a roll-up from Robert Kaufman, designed by Karen Lewis, called Blueberry Park. When giving yardage requirements for the sashing, we allowed a little extra so these strips can be cut lengthways. It only uses a small amount of extra fabric and we felt it was better not to have joins in the sashing and border strips. We generally avoid wastage but in this instance we felt it was justified.

VITAL STATISTICS

Finished size: 54in x 73in

YOU WILL NEED

- One jelly roll (or forty 2½in x width of fabric strips from your stash)

- 2yds (1.8m) of fabric for sashing and border

- The scrappy binding is made from left-over jelly roll strips

PREPARATION AND CUTTING

SORTING THE JELLY ROLL STRIPS

Sorting the colours is the most important part of this quilt as you want your colours to blend into each other and shade from dark to light. Choose thirty-three strips and sort them according to how you want them to be sewn together. Put the remaining seven strips aside for the scrappy binding.

CUTTING THE SASHING AND BORDER FABRIC

Cut six 4in wide strips *lengthways* down the fabric. The remainder of the fabric is spare.

MAKING THE QUILT

STRIP PIECING

1 Working from dark to light, sew five jelly roll strips together down the long sides to form a strip unit, as shown in the diagram. Sew one strip in place, sewing in one direction, and add the next strip by sewing in the opposite direction, and so on. This will prevent the strip unit 'bowing'. Press towards the darker fabric.

2 Keeping your strips in your chosen order, repeat this process with all thirty-three jelly roll strips to make a total of seven strip units. Each strip unit should be 10½in deep at this stage. Note: The last strip unit will only have three strips and will measure 6½in.

3 Take each strip unit, trim off the selvedges and cut the unit into one 4½in segment, one 8½in segment and one 28½in segment.

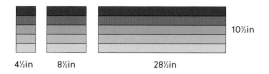

4 Sew all of the 4½in wide segments into a vertical row. Repeat with all the 8½in wide segments and then the 28½in wide segments, making sure that the fabrics are kept in the same order.

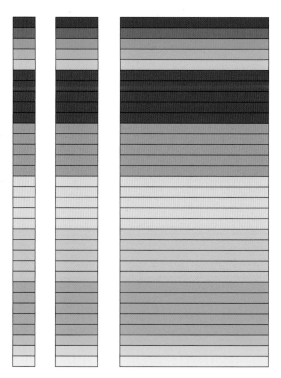

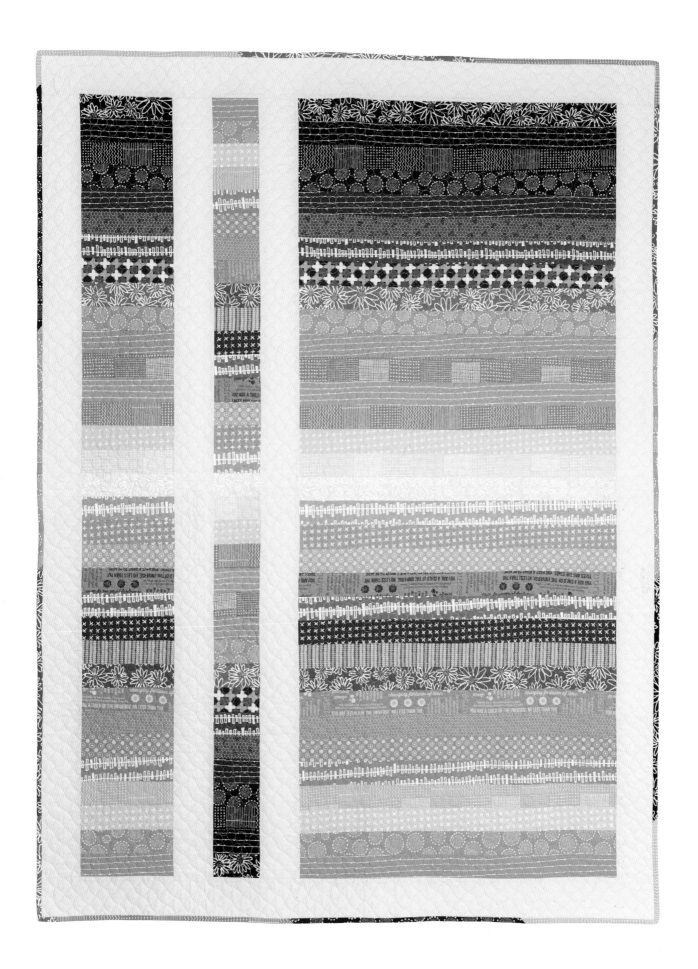

The quilt was made by the authors and long-arm quilted by The Quilt Room.

ADDING THE SASHING AND BORDERS

5 Measure the three vertical rows. They should of course all be the same but you never know! Your sashing/border strips must be the same length as the vertical rows, because your quilt will never be square if they are cut to different lengths. Rotate the 4½in vertical row 180 degrees and position it in between the 8½in row and 28½in row, as shown, in readiness for sewing.

6 Trim four sashing/border strips to the vertical measurement, making sure they are all the same length. Pin and sew the sashing/ border strips to the strip-pieced rows, easing the strips if necessary.

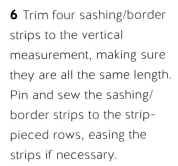

TIP: WHEN IT IS NECESSARY TO EASE FABRIC TO FIT, PLACE THE FABRIC THAT IS LONGER ON THE BOTTOM, BECAUSE THIS WILL ALLOW THE FEED DOGS TO HELP WITH THE EASING.

7 Now sew the sashing and vertical rows together and add a border strip at each side.

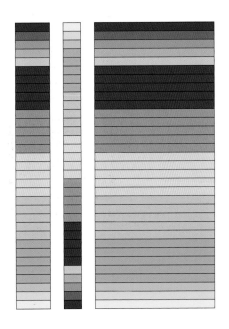

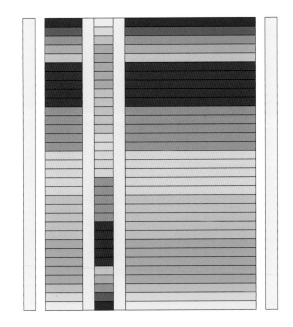

8 Determine the horizontal measurement from side to side across the centre of the quilt top. Trim two border strips to this measurement. Sew these to the top and bottom of the quilt, pinning and easing where necessary. Your quilt top is now complete.

QUILTING AND FINISHING

9 Make a quilt sandwich of the quilt top, the wadding (batting) and the backing. Quilt as desired and then bind to finish (see General Techniques: Binding a Quilt). To make a scrappy binding, cut each of the seven jelly roll strips allocated for the binding into two rectangles 2½in x 20in. Mix up these rectangles and then join them all together into a continuous length to make your scrappy binding.

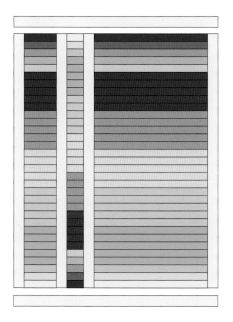

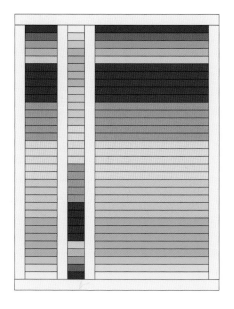

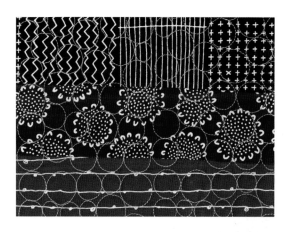

SCARLET STEPS

This is a very easy quilt and you will get it pieced in a weekend, however many tea breaks you have! The only time you have to match a seam is when sewing the rows together. The jelly roll does need to be one that has a distinct difference between light and dark as the design is dependent upon that. Artistic licence can be used when allocating lights and darks but if you don't have sufficient lights, then add an extra long quarter of light fabric. We used a jelly roll by Minick & Simpson called Miss Scarlet, which had more lights than darks, so we needed a long quarter of a dark red to help us out!

VITAL STATISTICS

Finished size: 60in x 62in

Block size: 6in x 10in (finished)

Number of blocks: 40

Setting: 8 x 5 blocks, plus 6in border (finished)

YOU WILL NEED

- One jelly roll (or forty 2½in x width of fabric strips from your stash)

- 1¼yds (1.10m) of border fabric

- The scrappy binding is made from excess jelly roll strips

PREPARATION AND CUTTING

SORTING THE JELLY ROLL STRIPS

Divide the jelly roll into twenty lights and twenty darks. Artistic licence can be used here but remember that it is the light and dark construction of the block that makes the design work.

CUTTING THE JELLY ROLL STRIPS

Cut each of the forty jelly roll strips into the following pieces.

- Two 2½in squares.
- Two 2½in x 5½in rectangles.
- Two 2½in x 8½in rectangles.

Set the remainder of each strip aside (approximately 2½in x 9in) for the scrappy binding.

For speedy cutting you can layer four strips (still folded) on top of each other, making sure the edges are aligned. Repeat and layer all your twenty lights strips (still folded) into five sets of four layered strips. Butt them up against each other with the left side aligned. Using a large quilting ruler or quilting square, trim the selvedge on the left and then cut one 2½in strip, one 5½in strip and one 8½in strip. This will give you two each of all twenty light rectangles in no time at all, with the balance of the strips set aside for the scrappy binding. Repeat with your dark strips.

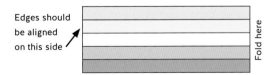

Edges should be aligned on this side

Fold here

CUTTING THE BORDER FABRIC

Cut six 6½in wide strips across the width of the fabric.

MAKING THE QUILT

SEWING THE BLOCKS

1 Take one light 2½in square and sew it to the right-hand side of a 2½in x 8½in dark rectangle. Press in the direction shown by the arrow in the diagram. Repeat to make forty of Unit A. Chain piecing will speed up the process.

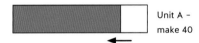

Unit A – make 40

2 Take a 2½in x 5½in light rectangle and sew it to the right-hand side of a 2½in x 5½in dark rectangle. Press in the direction shown by the arrow. Repeat to make forty of Unit B, chain piecing for speed.

Unit B – make 40

3 Take a 2½in dark square and sew it to the left-hand side of a 2½in x 8½in light rectangle. Press as shown. Repeat to make a total of forty of Unit C.

Unit C – make 40

4 Take one Unit A and one Unit B and sew together as shown. Repeat with all forty Unit A and forty Unit B. We didn't sort our units before sewing but we tried not to sew the same fabrics next to each other. There is no need to press yet.

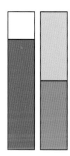

5 Take one Unit C and sew it to Units A/B. Repeat with all forty Unit C. Press as shown.

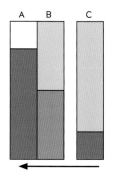

6 You now have forty blocks, each measuring 6½in x 10½in.

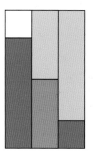

ASSEMBLING THE QUILT

7 Referring to the diagram, lay out the blocks into five rows of eight blocks each. When you are happy with the layout, sew the blocks together to form rows and then sew the rows together. When sewing the rows together, pin at all seam intersections to ensure a perfect match. This is the only time that you actually have to match a seam when making this quilt.

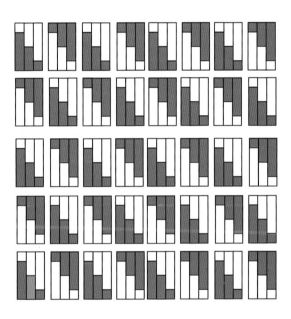

ADDING THE BORDER

8 Sew the six border strips end to end into a continuous length. Press seams open. Determine the vertical measurement from top to bottom through the centre of your quilt top. Cut two side borders to this measurement. Pin and sew to the quilt, easing if necessary.

9 Determine the horizontal measurement from side to side across the centre of the quilt top, including the two side borders. Cut two border strips to this measurement. Pin and sew to the top and bottom of the quilt. Press towards the border fabric. Your quilt top is now complete.

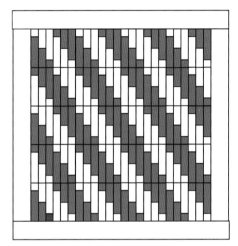

QUILTING AND FINISHING

10 Make a quilt sandwich of the quilt top, the wadding (batting) and the backing. Quilt as desired and bind to finish (see General Techniques: Binding a Quilt).

11 To make a scrappy binding, join the 2½in x 9in rectangles allocated for the binding into a continuous length, pressing seams open. You will need a total sewn length of about 270in. Press this strip in half all along the length, wrong sides together, so it's ready to use as the binding.

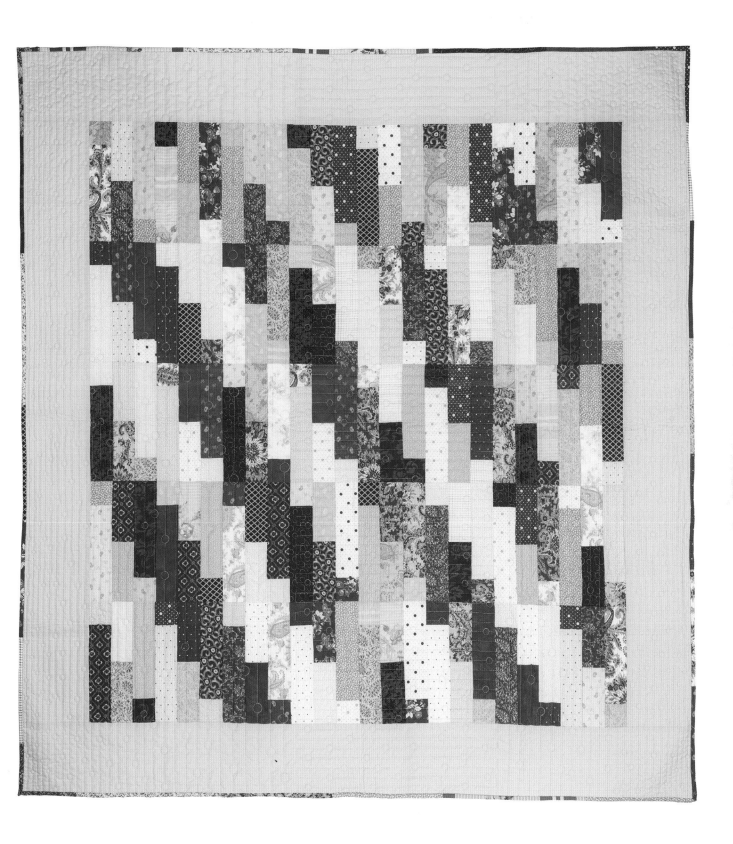

The quilt was made by the authors and long-arm quilted by The Quilt Room.

SKYLINE

If you need a quilt in a hurry – maybe a charity quilt or just a present that should have been started weeks ago – then this design is a good choice. It is very quick to put together, and easy too as there are no seams to match. We hope you agree that the end result looks great! Thanks to the simple design, the fabrics in the jelly roll are shown in all their glory and you only have to choose a background fabric. We used a jelly roll by Kate Spain for Moda, set against a lovely dark navy background that showed the fabrics off beautifully.

VITAL STATISTICS

Finished size: 62in x 74in

YOU WILL NEED

- One jelly roll (or forty 2½in strips cut across the width of the fabric)

- 1¾yds (1.5m) of background fabric

- The scrappy binding is made from left-over jelly roll strips

PREPARATION AND CUTTING

SORTING THE JELLY ROLL STRIPS

Choose thirty-three jelly roll strips for the quilt and use the remaining seven strips for the scrappy binding.

CUTTING THE BACKGROUND FABRIC

- Cut seventeen 2½in strips across the width of the fabric and sub-cut each into two rectangles approximately 2½in x 21in to make thirty-four rectangles. You need thirty-three so one is spare.

- Cut three 4½in strips across the width of the fabric for the top and bottom borders.

MAKING THE QUILT

SEWING THE PIECED STRIPS

1 Take one 2½in x 21in background rectangle and cut it into two rectangles. These can be random cuts as that is the nature of the design. For example, to start off you could cut it into two equal rectangles approximately 2½in x 11½in.

2 Sew one rectangle to one end of a jelly roll strip and the other rectangle to the other end. Press towards the background fabric.

3 Take a second 2½in x 21in background rectangle and cut it into two rectangles. This time do not cut them in half to create equal rectangles but make the cut in a different place to create two different size rectangles.

4 Sew one rectangle to one end of a jelly roll strip and the other rectangle to the other end. Press towards the background fabric.

5 Repeat this process with all thirty-three 2½in x 21in background rectangles and the thirty-three jelly roll strips.

TIP: YOU DO NOT NEED TO WORRY TOO MUCH ABOUT WHERE TO CUT YOUR BACKGROUND RECTANGLES AS YOU CAN PLAY AROUND WITH THE PLACEMENT OF THE ROWS WHEN THEY ARE ALL FINISHED.

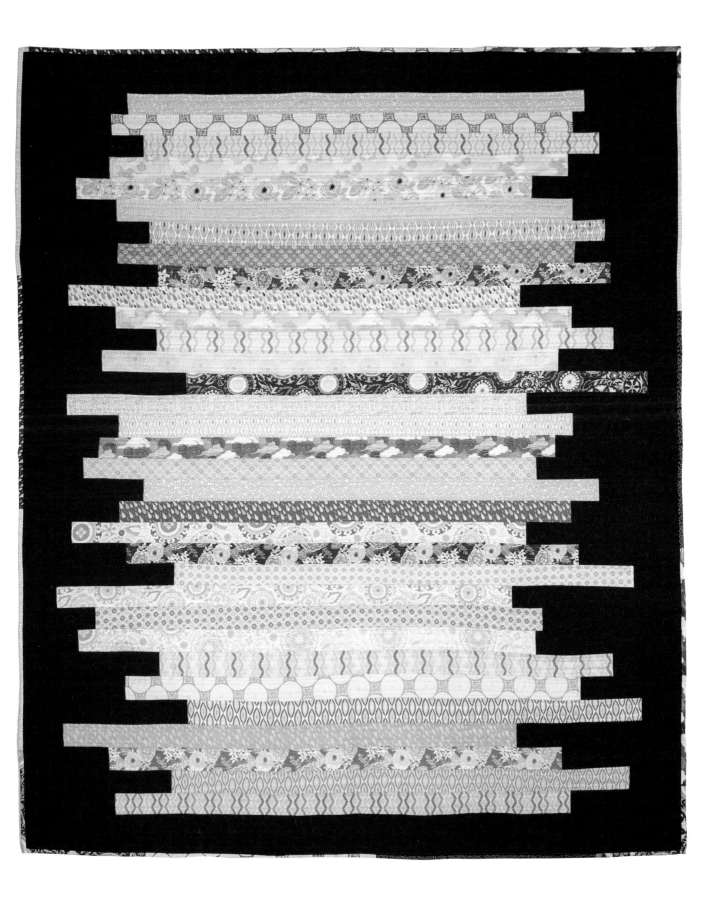

The quilt was made by the authors and long-arm quilted by The Quilt Room.

ASSEMBLING THE QUILT

6 Lay out the thirty-three rows in an order that looks pleasing and when you are happy with the layout, sew the rows together. The rows will vary in length slightly so when sewing them together make sure you keep one side even and then you will only have to trim one side, if necessary. Press the seams in one direction as shown.

ADDING THE BORDER

7 Sew all three 4½in border strips together in a continuous length and then cut in half to create two border strips of the same length. Measure the width of the quilt and trim the border strips to the exact size. Pin and sew to the top and bottom of the quilt.

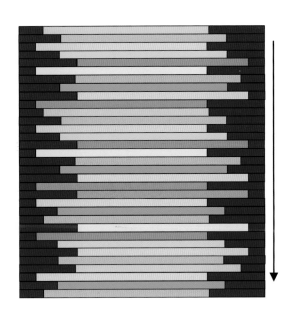

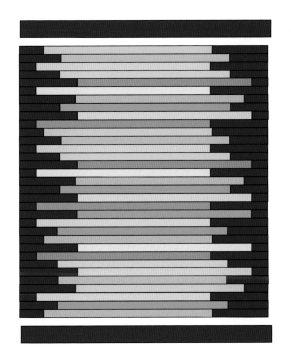

8 Using a long quilting ruler, trim the sides of the quilt to create a straight edge, if necessary. Your quilt top is now complete.

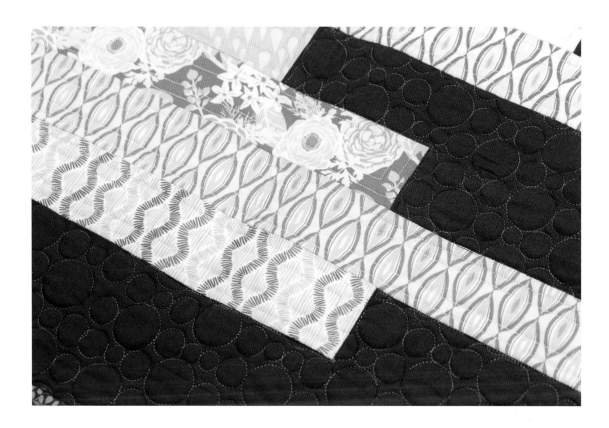

QUILTING AND FINISHING

9 Make a quilt sandwich of the quilt top, the wadding (batting) and the backing. Quilt as desired and bind to finish (see General Techniques: Binding a Quilt).

10 To create a scrappy binding, cut each of the binding strips into two rectangles, mix them up and then sew them all together into a continuous length, pressing seams open. Press this length in half along the length, wrong sides together, so it's ready to use as the binding.

SPRINGTIME IN PARIS

This is a fun quilt to make, with an interesting slanting star pattern created by the piecing. It goes together quickly so you can really see your quilt taking shape before your eyes – very rewarding! We used one of our own Quilt Room strip rolls. The one used for this quilt contained a variety of prints, mostly Anna Griffin fabrics but with a few others added in to really make it shine. For our border and accent fabric we used a solid dark taupe, which we think sets the fabrics off to their best advantage.

VITAL STATISTICS

Finished size: 52in x 64in

Block size: 6in square (finished)

Number of blocks: 63

Setting: 7 x 9 blocks, plus 5in border (finished)

YOU WILL NEED

- One jelly roll (or forty 2½in x width of fabric strips from your stash)

- 2¼yds (2m) of accent and border fabric

- The scrappy binding is made from left-over jelly roll strips

PREPARATION AND CUTTING

SORTING THE JELLY ROLL STRIPS

Choose thirty-three jelly roll strips for the blocks. Reserve the remainder for the scrappy binding.

CUTTING THE ACCENT AND BORDER FABRIC

- Cut eleven 3½in wide strips across the width of the fabric and sub-cut each into twelve 3½in squares for a total of 132 squares. You need 126, so six are spare.

- Cut six 5½in wide strips across the width of the fabric and set these aside for the border.

MAKING THE QUILT

MAKING THE STRIP UNITS

1 Choose three jelly roll strips and sew them together down the long sides to form a strip unit. Sew one strip in one direction and one in the other and this will prevent the strip units from 'bowing'. Press the strips in one direction, as shown by the diagram arrow.

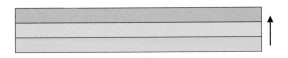

2 Repeat with all thirty-three jelly roll strips to make a total of eleven strip units.

3 Take one strip unit, trim off the selvedge and cut the unit into six 6½in squares.

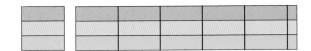

4 Repeat with all eleven strip units to make a total of sixty-six 6½in squares. You need sixty-three squares, so three will be spare.

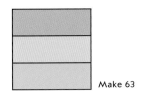

Make 63

5 Take one 3½in accent square and draw a diagonal line from corner to corner on the wrong side.

6 With right sides together, lay a marked 3½in square on the top left corner of a 6½in pieced square, making sure the strips are horizontal and the outer edges are aligned. Sew across the diagonal, using the marked diagonal line as the stitching line.

7 Flip the square over and press towards the outside of the block. Trim the excess fabric from the snowball corner but do not trim the pieced block fabric as this helps keep your patchwork in shape (see Tip).

TIP: WHEN MAKING THE SNOWBALL CORNERS, IF YOU FIND THE WORK TOO BULKY AT THE CORNERS AND WISH TO TRIM THE STRIP-PIECED BLOCK AS WELL, DO NOT TRIM THIS UNTIL YOU ARE ABSOLUTELY SURE YOUR SNOWBALL CORNER IS SEWN ON ACCURATELY.

8 Repeat this process to add another 3½in square on the opposite corner. After a while you may find you do not need to mark the sewing line as it is not difficult to judge the line. Alternatively, you can mark the line with a fold. Repeat this process to make sixty-three blocks in total.

ASSEMBLING THE QUILT

9 Lay out your blocks into nine rows of seven blocks. When you are happy with the layout sew the blocks into rows. Press alternate rows in opposite directions. Now sew the rows together, pinning at all seam intersections, and then press.

ADDING THE BORDER

10 Sew your six 5½in border strips into a continuous length and press seams open.

11 Determine the vertical measurement from top to bottom through the centre of your quilt top. Cut two side borders to this measurement. Pin and sew to the quilt, easing if necessary.

12 Determine the horizontal measurement from side to side across the centre of the quilt top. Cut two border strips to this measurement. Pin and sew to the top and bottom of the quilt. Press towards the border fabric. Your quilt top is now complete.

QUILTING AND FINISHING

13 Make a quilt sandwich of the quilt top, the wadding (batting) and the backing. Quilt as desired and then bind to finish (see General Techniques: Binding a Quilt).

14 To make a scrappy binding, cut each of the jelly roll strips allocated for the binding into two rectangles 2½in x 21in. Join them into a continuous length, pressing seams open. Press this length in half all along the length, wrong sides together, so it's ready to use as the binding.

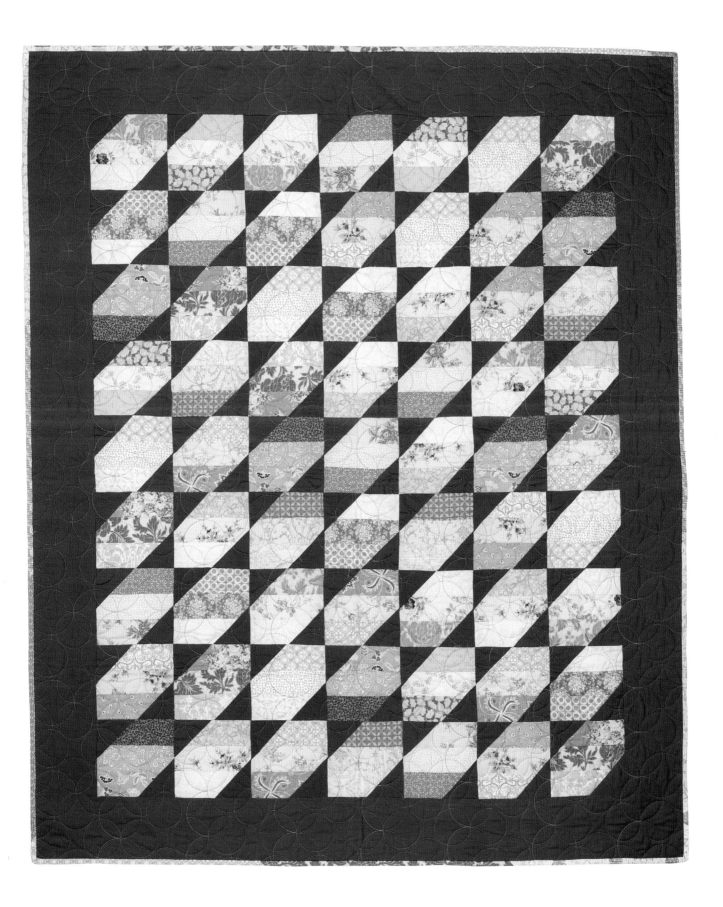

The quilt was made by the authors and long-arm quilted by The Quilt Room.

FRUIT PUNCH

This is a lovely quilt to put together as everything seems to fall into place easily. There is a little more piecing than in the previous quilts but strip piecing hugely speeds up this process. We used a bright, colourful jelly roll called Little Ruby from Bonnie & Camille for Moda, which had a gorgeous mix of reds, pinks, greens and aquas, combining this with a crisp white background fabric. The block is a simple four-patch with border, but setting the blocks on point makes the squares look like diamonds, creating a more complicated-looking design.

VITAL STATISTICS

Finished size: 58in x 69in

Block size: 8in square (finished)

Number of blocks: 50

Setting: on point

YOU WILL NEED

- One jelly roll (or forty 2½in x width of fabric strips from your stash)

- 2yds (1.8m) of background fabric

- ½yd (50cm) of binding fabric (see Tip overleaf)

PREPARATION AND CUTTING

SORTING THE JELLY ROLL STRIPS

- Select thirty strips for the outer frames of block A. These strips will also make the four-patch units.

- Select four strips to make extra four-patch units.

- Six jelly roll strips will be spare (see Tip).

CUTTING THE JELLY ROLL STRIPS

Leave the four strips allocated for the extra four-patch units uncut.

Cut each of the thirty jelly roll strips allocated for the outer frames as follows (keeping the 2½in x 4½in rectangles and the 2½in x 8½in rectangles from the same fabric together).

- Two 2½in x 4½in rectangles.

- Two 2½in x 8½in rectangles.

- One 2½in x 16in rectangle for the four-patch units.

CUTTING THE BACKGROUND FABRIC

Cut fifteen 2½in wide strips across the width of the fabric.

- Take five strips and sub-cut each into eight 2½in x 4½in rectangles to make a total of forty rectangles.

- Take ten strips and sub-cut each into four 2½in x 8½in rectangles to make a total of forty rectangles.

Cut two 13½in wide strips across the width of the fabric.

- Sub-cut one strip into three 13½in squares and one strip into two 13½in squares and two 7½in squares.

- Take the five 13½in squares and cut across both diagonals to form twenty setting triangles. You need eighteen so two are spare.

- Take the two 7½in squares and cut across one diagonal of these squares to form four corner triangles. Cutting the setting and corner triangles in this way ensures that there are no bias edges on the outside of your quilt.

13½in square   7½in square

TIP: IF YOU PREFER, YOU COULD USE THE SIX SPARE JELLY ROLL STRIPS AND ADD ONE MORE STRIP TO MAKE A SCRAPPY BINDING, INSTEAD OF BUYING A SINGLE FABRIC FOR THE BINDING.

MAKING THE QUILT

MAKING THE FOUR-PATCH UNITS

1 Choose two contrasting 2½in x 16in jelly roll rectangles and lay them right sides together. Sew down the long side. Open and press towards the darker fabric. Repeat with twenty-eight of the 2½in x 16in rectangles (two are spare) to make a total of fourteen strip units, chain piecing for speed. Open and press towards the darker fabric.

Make 14

2 With right sides together, lay one strip unit on top of another, with the lighter strip on the top of one unit and on the bottom of another, ensuring that the centre seams are in alignment.

3 Sub-cut these paired units into six 2½in wide segments.

4 Carefully keeping the pairs together, sew down the long side as shown, pinning at the seam intersection to ensure a perfect match. The seams will nest together nicely because they are pressed in different directions. Chain piece when you can, for speed. Press open to form six four-patch units.

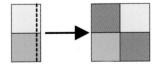

5 Repeat this process (steps 2–4) with all fourteen strip units to make forty-two four-patch units.

6 Using the four jelly roll strips allocated for the extra four-patch units, repeat this process (steps 1–4) to make a further eight four-patch units. You should now have fifty assorted four-patch units.

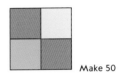

Make 50

MAKING BLOCK A

7 Choose thirty of the four-patch units for block A. These will have the jelly roll fabrics as borders.

8 Working with pieces from the same jelly roll strip, take one four-patch unit and sew a 2½in x 4½in rectangle to both sides. Press the seams away from the four-patch unit.

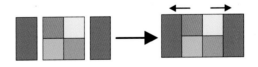

9 Sew a 2½in x 8½in rectangle of the same fabric to the top and bottom of this unit. Press as shown.

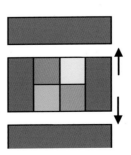

10 Repeat to make thirty of block A. Chain piecing will speed up this process.

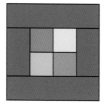

Make 30 of Block A

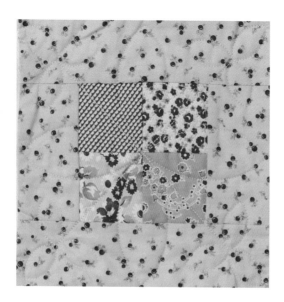

MAKING BLOCK B

11 Working with the twenty remaining four-patch units, sew a 2½in x 4½in background rectangle to both sides. Press the seams away from the four-patch unit.

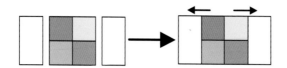

12 Sew a 2½in x 8½in background rectangle to the top and bottom of this unit. Press the seams as shown.

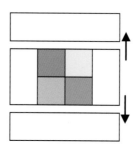

13 Repeat to make twenty of block B, chain piecing for speed.

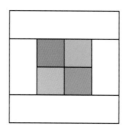

Make 20 of Block B

The quilt was made by the authors and long-arm quilted by The Quilt Room.

ASSEMBLING THE QUILT

14 Referring to the piecing diagram, lay out your blocks with a setting triangle at each end. Lay the A blocks with the seams vertical and the B blocks with the seams horizontal.

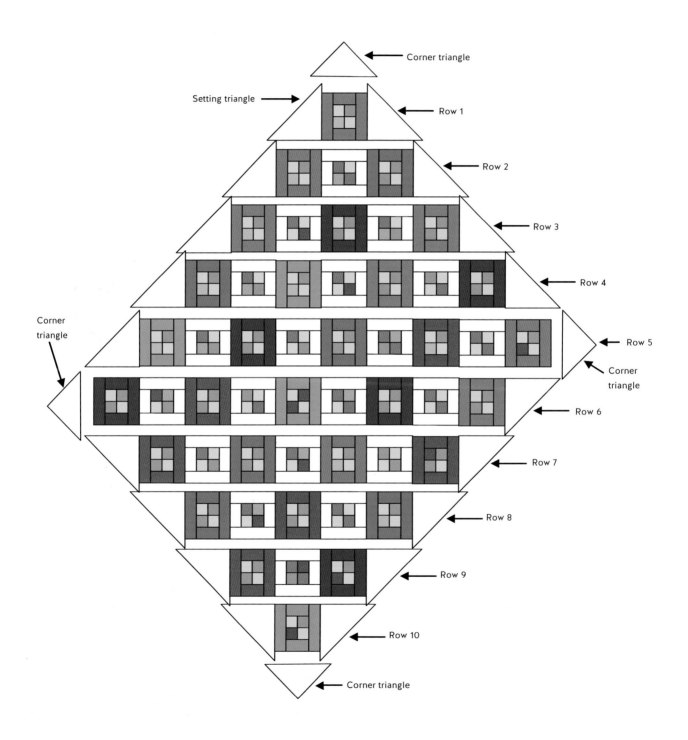

15 When you are happy with the layout, create row 1 by sewing a setting triangle to both sides of a block A. The setting triangles have been cut slightly larger to make the blocks 'float', so when sewing the triangles make sure the bottom of the triangle is aligned with the block. Press as shown.

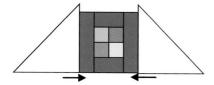

16 Continue to sew the blocks together to form rows with setting triangles at each end. Always press the seams towards block A to ensure that the blocks nest together nicely when the rows are sewn together.

17 Now sew the rows together, pinning at every intersection. Sew the corner triangles on last. Your quilt top is now complete.

QUILTING AND FINISHING

18 Make a quilt sandwich of the quilt top, the wadding (batting) and the backing. Quilt as desired and bind to finish (see General Techniques: Binding a Quilt).

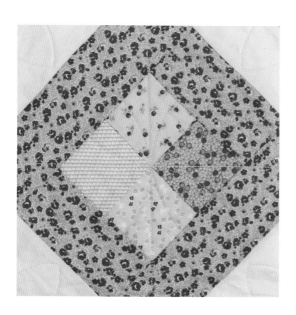

SUNDIAL

This is a clever design that creates such a lovely effect. You need to be able to divide your jelly roll into either lights or darks or into two different colourways, as this creates the design. Artistic licence can be used here but there definitely needs to be a distinction between the two. We used a French General jelly roll called Ville Fleurie, which had gorgeous reds and purples used as our darks, plus a sufficient number of interesting lights. We used a red Grunge fabric from Moda for our border, which we felt gave the right effect.

VITAL STATISTICS

Finished size: 55in square

Block size: 11in square (finished)

Number of blocks: 16

Setting: 4 x 4 blocks, plus 5½in border (finished)

YOU WILL NEED

- One jelly roll (or forty 2½in x width of fabric strips from your stash)

- 1yd (90cm) of border fabric

- ½yd (50cm) of binding fabric

PREPARATION AND CUTTING

SORTING THE JELLY ROLL STRIPS

Divide your jelly roll into eighteen light strips and eighteen dark strips, or eighteen of one colour and eighteen of another. Artistic licence can be used here.

Now sort the strips into six sets of three dark strips each and six sets of three light strips each. Four of your jelly roll strips will be spare.

CUTTING THE BORDER FABRIC

Cut five 6in strips across the width of the fabric.

CUTTING THE BINDING FABRIC

Cut six 2½in wide strips across the width of fabric.

MAKING THE QUILT

MAKING THE BLOCKS

1 Sew one set of three dark strips together along their length. Check that the width of your sewn strip unit is 6½in. If not, adjust your seam allowance. Press the seams in one direction as shown by the arrow in the diagram. Repeat with all six sets of dark strips to make six dark strip units.

TIP: SITTING FOR A LONG TIME AT YOUR SEWING MACHINE IS NOT GOOD FOR YOU, SO MAKE SURE YOU GET UP AND WANDER AROUND OCCASIONALLY. OUR TRICK IS TO KEEP OUR IRONING BOARD WELL AWAY FROM OUR SEWING MACHINE SO AT LEAST WE GET SOME EXERCISE DURING THE DAY!

2 Repeat with the six sets of light strips to make six light strip units. Press the seams in one direction as shown.

3 Lay one light strip unit on top of one dark strip unit, aligning the edges and nesting the seams up against each other carefully.

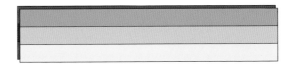

4 Cut the pair of strip units into six pairs of 6½in squares. You will get six pairs per strip unit.

5 Carefully keeping the pairs together, draw a diagonal line from *bottom right to top left* on all six pairs of squares.

6 Pin to hold the pairs in position and stitch both sides of the drawn line with a scant ¼in seam allowance.

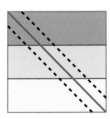

7 Press the stitches to set them and then cut the unit into two units along the drawn diagonal line.

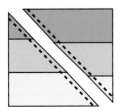

8 Trim dog ears and press open towards the dark fabric. These are Unit A. You will get twelve Unit As from one pair of strip units. Label these units as A. Note: there are two different units but the important thing is the placement of the light and dark triangles and the direction of the seams.

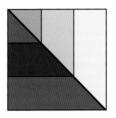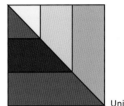

Unit A

9 Repeat with another two pairs of light and dark strip units to make a total of thirty-six unit As (the extra units will allow you some choice when assembling the quilt).

10 Repeat this process (steps 3–9) with the remaining three pairs of strip units, but this time draw the diagonal line from *bottom left to top right* on the squares.

11 Press the stitches to set them and then cut along the drawn diagonal line.

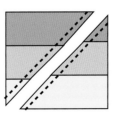

12 Trim dog ears and press open towards the dark fabric. These are Unit B. You will have a total of thirty-six Unit B (the extra units will allow you some choice when assembling the quilt). Label these units as B. Note: there are two different units but the important thing is the placement of the light and dark triangles and the direction of the seams.

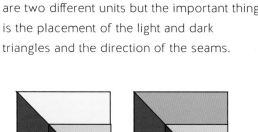

Unit B

ASSEMBLING THE QUILT

13 Take two A units and two B units and sew them together to form the pinwheel block as shown. We placed two unit As with the same fabric in each block, with two unit Bs with the same fabric. These blocks can be as scrappy as you like or you can make them more coordinated if you prefer. Notice the dark strips are all horizontal and the light strips are all vertical.

14 Repeat this process to make a total of sixteen large pinwheel blocks. You will have eight units spare.

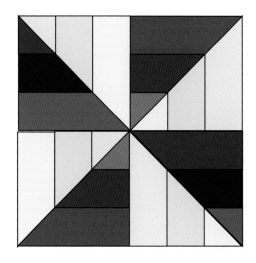

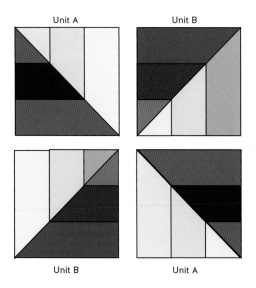

Unit A	Unit B
Unit B	Unit A

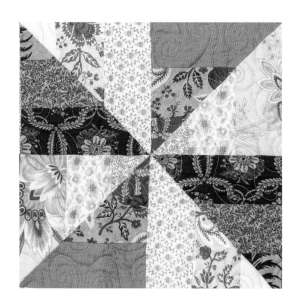

The quilt was made by the authors and long-arm quilted by The Quilt Room.

15 Lay out the blocks into four rows of four large pinwheel blocks. When you are happy with the layout, sew the blocks into rows, pressing alternate rows in opposite directions, so seams will nest together. Now sew the rows together, pinning at every seam intersection to ensure a perfect match, and press.

ADDING THE BORDER

16 Sew the six border strips together end to end into a continuous length, pressing seams open.

17 Determine the vertical measurement from top to bottom through the centre of your quilt top. Cut two side borders to this measurement. Pin and sew to the quilt, easing if necessary.

18 Determine the horizontal measurement from side to side across the centre of the quilt top, including the borders just added. Cut two border strips to this measurement. Pin and sew to the top and bottom of the quilt. Press towards the border fabric. Your quilt top is now complete.

QUILTING AND FINISHING

19 Make a quilt sandwich of the quilt top, the wadding (batting) and the backing. Quilt as desired and then bind to finish (see General Techniques: Binding a Quilt).

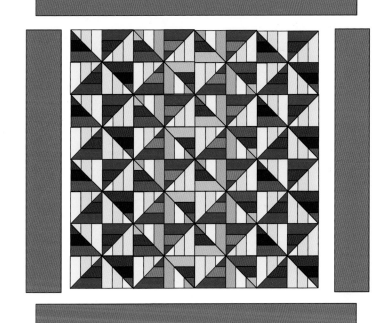

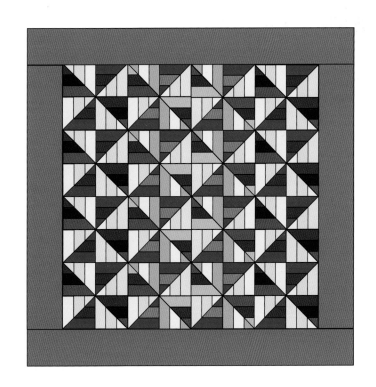

NORWEGIAN WOOD

If you don't normally chain piece, then this is a great quilt to get some practice! There are lots of pieces but it's amazing how quickly it goes together with chain piecing. There's also very little pinning as it is only necessary to use one pin when sewing the rows of the blocks together. Some of the strips in the quilt need to measure at least 42½in, particularly the aqua and apricot colourways (rows A and E) so don't be too zealous when trimming selvedges. We used delightful Tilda fabrics from the Cabbage Rose and Memory Lane ranges. Designed by Tone Finnanger, these fabrics always look so fresh and colourful.

VITAL STATISTICS

Finished size: 60in square

Block size: 10in square (finished)

Number of blocks: 36

Setting: 3 x 3 blocks

YOU WILL NEED

- One jelly roll (or forty 2½in x width of fabric strips from your stash)

- 1yd (90cm) of cream accent fabric

- ½yd (50cm) of binding fabric

PREPARATION AND CUTTING

SORTING THE JELLY ROLL STRIPS

Divide the jelly roll into five colourways – we used aqua for row A, pink for row B, blue for row C, green for row D and apricot for row E. Artistic licence can be used here but you need eight strips in each colourway.

CUTTING THE AQUA COLOURWAY (ROW A)

Cut each of the eight aqua strips into five 2½in x 8½in rectangles to make a total of forty. You need thirty-six so four are spare. Note: you need a strip length of 42½in for this so be careful not to trim selvedges excessively.

CUTTING THE PINK COLOURWAY (ROW B)

- Take six pink strips and cut each strip into six 2½in x 6½in rectangles plus one 2½in square.

- Take two pink strips and cut each strip into sixteen 2½in squares.

- You need thirty-six 2½in x 6½in rectangles and thirty-six 2½in squares (you will have two spare).

CUTTING THE BLUE COLOURWAY (ROW C)

Cut each of the eight blue strips into nine 2½in x 4½in rectangles. You need a total of seventy-two.

CUTTING THE GREEN COLOURWAY (ROW D)

- Take six green strips and cut each strip into six 2½in x 6½in rectangles plus one 2½in square.

- Take two green strips and cut each strip into sixteen 2½in squares.

- You need thirty-six 2½in x 6½in rectangles and thirty-six 2½in squares (two are spare).

CUTTING THE APRICOT COLOURWAY (ROW E)

Cut each of the eight apricot strips into five 2½in x 8½in rectangles to make a total of forty. You need thirty-six so four are spare. Note: you need a strip length of 42½in for this so don't trim selvedges excessively.

CUTTING THE ACCENT FABRIC

Cut twelve 2½in wide strips across the width of the fabric and sub-cut each strip into sixteen 2½in squares to make a total of 192. You need 180, so you will have twelve spare.

CUTTING THE BINDING FABRIC

Cut six 2½in wide strips across the width of the fabric.

TIP: WE OPTED FOR A LIGHT ACCENT FABRIC FOR OUR 'CHAIN' TO KEEP THE QUILT LIGHT AND AIRY. A DARK FABRIC WOULD MAKE THE CHAIN MORE DOMINANT IF YOU PREFER.

MAKING THE QUILT

SEWING ROW A

1 Sew a 2½in accent square to the left of a 2½in x 8½in aqua rectangle to make row A. Repeat to make thirty-six row A, chain piecing for speed. Press away from the accent square as shown.

Row A – make 36

SEWING ROW B

2 Sew a 2½in accent square to the left-hand side of a 2½in x 6½in pink rectangle. Repeat with all thirty-six 2½in x 6½in pink rectangles, chain piecing for speed.

3 Sew a 2½in pink square to the left-hand side of this unit to make row B. Repeat to make thirty-six row B. Press away from the accent square as shown.

Row B – make 36

SEWING ROW C

4 Sew a 2½in accent square to the left-hand side of a 2½in x 4½in blue rectangle. Repeat with thirty-six 2½in x 4½in blue rectangles.

5 Sew a 2½in x 4½in blue rectangle to the left-hand side of this unit to make row C. Repeat to make thirty-six row C. Press away from the accent square, as shown.

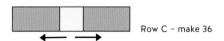

Row C – make 36

SEWING ROW D

6 Sew a 2½in accent square to the right-hand side of a 2½in x 6½in green rectangle. Repeat with all thirty-six 2½in x 6½in green rectangles.

7 Sew a 2½in green square to the right-hand side of this unit to make row D. Repeat to make thirty-six row D. Press away from the accent square.

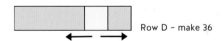

Row D – make 36

SEWING ROW E

8 Sew a 2½in accent square to the right-hand side of a 2½in x 8½in apricot rectangle to make row E. Repeat to make thirty-six row E. Press away from the accent square.

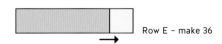

Row E – make 36

ASSEMBLING THE BLOCKS

9 Take one row A and one row B and sew together as shown, pinning at the seam intersection to ensure a perfect match. You will see that only one pin is needed at the seam intersection. Repeat with all thirty-six row A and thirty-six row B, chain piecing for speed. Press the units as shown.

10 Take the thirty-six of row C and chain piece to the bottom of these units, pinning at the seam intersection to ensure a perfect match. Press the units as shown.

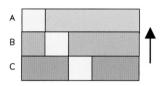

11 Take the thirty-six of row D and chain piece to the bottom of these units, pinning at the seam intersection to ensure a perfect match. Press the units as shown.

12 Take the thirty-six of row E and chain piece to the bottom of these units, pinning at the seam intersection to ensure a perfect match. Press as shown. Your thirty-six blocks are now complete.

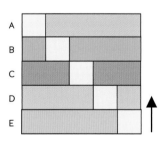

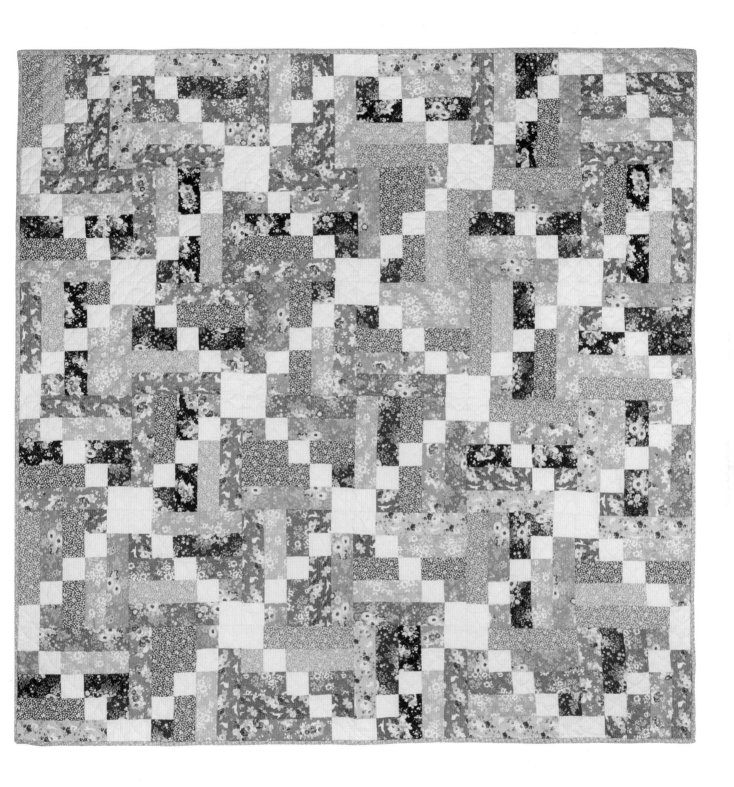

The quilt was made by the authors and long-arm quilted by The Quilt Room.

ASSEMBLING THE QUILT

13 Take four blocks and rotate them to make the pattern shown in the diagram. Sew them together, pinning at the seam intersections to ensure a perfect match. Repeat with all thirty-six blocks to make nine larger units. Press as shown.

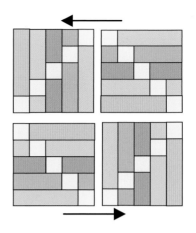

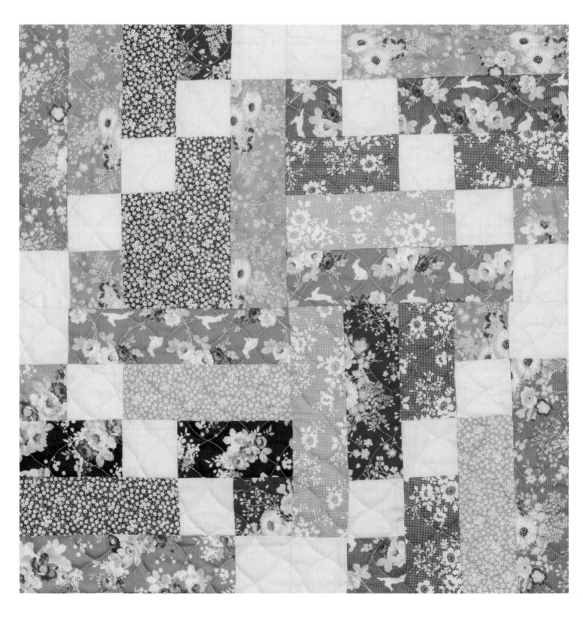

14 Sew the larger units into three rows of three units each, pinning at all seam intersections to ensure a perfect match. Press well. Your quilt top is now complete.

QUILTING AND FINISHING

15 Make a quilt sandwich of the quilt top, the wadding (batting) and the backing. Quilt as desired and bind to finish (see General Techniques: Binding a Quilt).

PICNIC TIME

We can imagine laying this quilt out on the lawn on a
summer's day – it would certainly have the wow factor!
You do need a large 60-degree triangle to make it but once
you've used it you will realise how many great designs you
can create with it. If you have a weekend to yourself the
piecing for this quilt goes together quickly and makes a
good single bed-size quilt – not to mention a picnic
blanket! We used a bright, zingy jelly roll called Garden
Project by Tim and Beck for Moda and matched it with a
gentle grey background fabric.

VITAL STATISTICS

Finished size: 60in x 72in

YOU WILL NEED

- One jelly roll (or forty 2½in x width of
  fabric strips from your stash)

- 3¼yds (3m) of background fabric

- ½yd (50cm) of binding fabric

- Large 60-degree triangle (at least 12½in)
  – we used a Creative Grids triangle

PREPARATION AND CUTTING

SORTING THE JELLY ROLL STRIPS

Sort the strips into twelve sets of three strips each – try to have different colours within the sets. This is a scrappy quilt and not a lot of thought has to be given to this! Four strips will be spare.

CUTTING THE BACKGROUND FABRIC

Cut nine 12½in strips across the width of the fabric and using a large 60-degree triangle ruler, sub-cut each strip into four 12½in 60-degree triangles (see diagram). You need thirty-six background triangles in total.

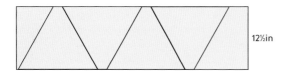

12½in

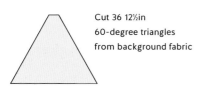

Cut 36 12½in
60-degree triangles
from background fabric

TIP: WHEN WORKING WITH JELLY ROLLS, LINT BUILDS UP IN THE BOBBIN CASE AND IT NEEDS TO BE CLEARED REGULARLY. YOU ALSO NEED TO CHANGE YOUR SEWING MACHINE NEEDLE REGULARLY TO GET THE BEST RESULTS.

MAKING THE QUILT

PREPARING THE TRIANGLE UNITS

1 Sew three jelly roll strips together, to make a strip unit, as shown in the diagram. Repeat to make twelve strip units in total.

2 Place the 60-degree triangle on the left side of the strip unit, aligning the 6½in line of the triangle with the bottom of the strip and the cut-off top of the triangle with the top of the strip. Cut the first triangle unit.

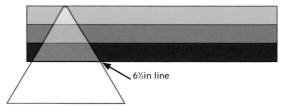

6½in line

3 Rotate the triangle 180 degrees and align the 6½in line with the top of the strip, as shown. Cut the second triangle unit. Continue rotating the ruler in this way to the end of the strip, cutting eight triangle units from the strip.

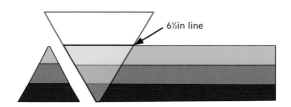

6½in line

4 Repeat with all twelve strip units to make ninety-six triangle units in total.

6 Sew another triangle to the top of the unit and press as shown.

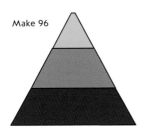

Make 96

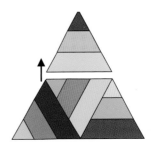

7 Repeat to make twenty-four larger triangles, taking care to keep the triangles facing the correct way.

SEWING THE TRIANGLE UNITS TOGETHER

5 Choose three assorted triangles and sew them together as shown. Press the seams towards the outside triangles.

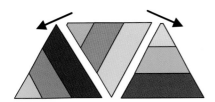

SEWING THE ROWS TOGETHER

8 To assemble the rows, sew four pieced triangles together with five background triangles to make one row. Press towards the background triangles.

9 Repeat this process to make six rows in total.

TIP: A FABRIC CUT WITH BIAS EDGES IS MORE PRONE TO STRETCHING, SO HANDLE CUT PIECES GENTLY AND PRESS PIECES CAREFULLY.

10 Lay out the rows as shown and when you are happy with the layout, sew an extra background triangle to the right-hand side of rows 1, 3, and 5 and to the left-hand side of rows 2, 4 and 6.

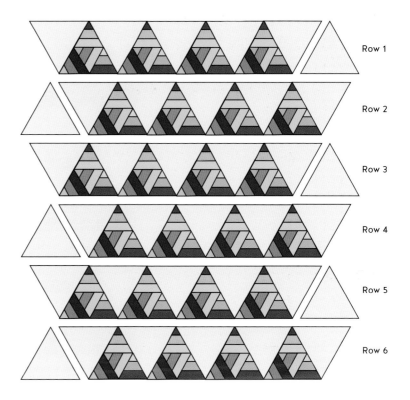

11 Sew the rows together as shown, pinning at the seam intersections to ensure a perfect match. Press the seams.

12 Using a long quilting ruler, trim the sides to straighten the edges of your quilt, allowing a ¼in seam allowance beyond the outside triangles so you do not lose the points of the triangles when the binding is attached. Your quilt top is now complete.

Trim the sides

QUILTING AND FINISHING

13 Make a quilt sandwich of the quilt top, the wadding (batting) and the backing. Quilt as desired and then bind to finish (see General Techniques: Binding a Quilt). If at this stage you find that one of your triangle units is facing in the wrong direction (as two of ours are!), you can always say that it was meant to be that way as no one is perfect!

The quilt was made by the authors and long-arm quilted by The Quilt Room.

BEACH LIFE

This quilt goes together beautifully with no wastage but you do need your strips to measure 42½in. Most strips measure up to 44in so this shouldn't be a problem but just be careful that you are not over-zealous when trimming the selvedges. The sixteen-patch blocks can be made quite quickly with good old strip piecing – what would we do without this efficient technique? We used the bright, clear colours from the Flow range by Zen Chic, with a background white-on-white from the Twist range by Dashwood Studio.

VITAL STATISTICS

Finished size: 58in square

Block size: 8in square (finished)

Number of blocks: 16

Setting: 4 x 4 blocks, plus 2in sashing, plus 8in piano keys border (finished)

YOU WILL NEED

- One jelly roll (or forty 2½in x width of fabric strips from your stash)

- ¾yd (70cm) of light fabric for sashing

- ½yd (50cm) of binding fabric

PREPARATION AND CUTTING

SORTING THE JELLY ROLL STRIPS

This is a scrappy quilt and there is very little sorting of fabrics needed. All forty strips are sewn into ten-strip units and at that stage five strip units are chosen for the blocks and five for the piano keys border. You could make it more coordinated if you prefer.

CUTTING THE LIGHT SASHING FABRIC

- Cut ten 2½in strips across the width of the fabric. Take five of these and sub-cut into 2½in x 8½in sashing rectangles. You need twenty.

- Set aside the remaining five 2½in wide strips for the horizontal sashing strips. Don't trim these to size until later, when you've checked the quilt centre measurement.

CUTTING THE BINDING FABRIC

Cut six 2½in wide strips across the width of the fabric.

TIP: MOST MODERN SEWING MACHINES HAVE A 'NEEDLE DOWN' OPTION, WHICH ENSURES THAT WHEN YOU STOP SEWING YOUR NEEDLE STOPS IN YOUR FABRIC. THIS PREVENTS UNNECESSARY MOVEMENT OF YOUR FABRIC AND KEEPS YOUR SEWING ACCURATE.

MAKING THE QUILT

SEWING THE STRIP UNITS

1 Choose four jelly roll strips and sew them together down the long side to create a strip unit. Sew the seams in opposite directions as this will prevent the strip unit from 'bowing'. Press the seams in one direction, as shown by the arrow in the diagram. Repeat to make ten strip units.

Make 10

2 Choose five of the strip units for use in the piano keys border and cut each of these strip units into five 8½in wide segments to make twenty-five 8½in squares. You need twenty-four so one is spare. Set these aside for the border. Note: do not be too zealous when trimming the selvedge as the strips need to measure 42½in.

Cut 5 strip units like this

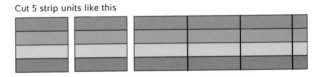

3 Take the remaining five strip units that will be used for the blocks and cut each strip unit into sixteen 2½in wide segments to make eighty 2½in wide segments.

Cut 5 strip units like this

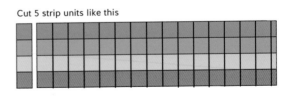

PIECING THE BLOCKS

4 Choose four assorted 2½in wide segments and sew them together, pinning at each seam intersection to ensure a perfect match. Be prepared to rotate units 180 degrees if necessary to make sure the seams are nesting together nicely before sewing. Press the sewn seams.

5 Repeat this process to make twenty blocks in total.

Make 20

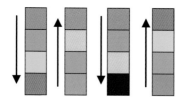

TIP: WE AIM TO HAVE AS LITTLE WASTAGE AS POSSIBLE FROM OUR JELLY ROLL STRIPS. IT IS THEREFORE IMPORTANT NOT TO BE TOO ZEALOUS WHEN TRIMMING SELVEDGES, PARTICULARLY FOR THIS QUILT.

ASSEMBLING THE QUILT

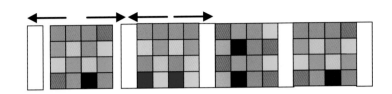

6 Sew four blocks together with a light 2½in x 8½in sashing rectangle in between and at each end. Repeat to make four rows. Press towards the sashing strips. Measure the width of the rows – they should measure 42½in.

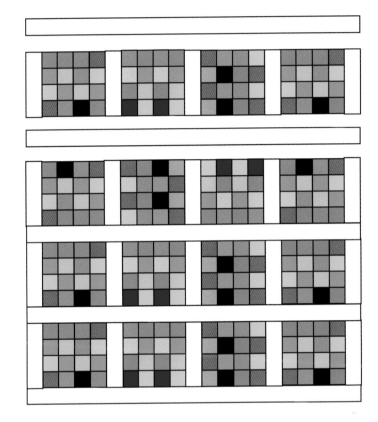

7 Trim the five 2½in strips set aside for the horizontal sashing to 42½in (or to your quilt's measurement if it is not 42½in). Sew the four rows of the quilt together with a sashing strip in between and also at the top and bottom, pinning and easing where necessary and then press.

The quilt was made by the authors and long-arm quilted by The Quilt Room.

MAKING THE PIANO KEYS BORDER

8 Sew six 8½in pieced squares together to make one border strip. You only need twenty-one segments for each border strip so you will have three extra. Unpick three segments from one end. Repeat this process to make four border strips.

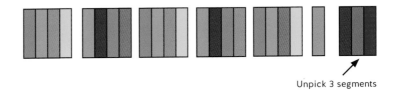

Unpick 3 segments

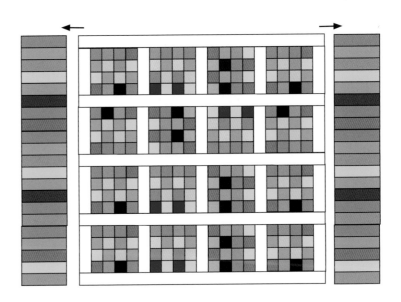

9 Pin and sew two border strips to the sides of the quilt, pinning and easing where necessary, and then press as shown.

10 Sew the remaining four pieced blocks to both ends of the remaining two border strips. Press towards the border strips.

11 Pin and sew these to the top and bottom of your quilt, easing where necessary, and then press. Your quilt top is now complete.

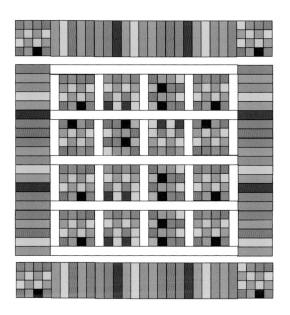 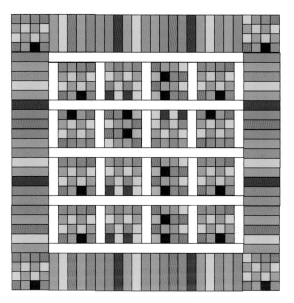

QUILTING AND FINISHING

12 Make a quilt sandwich of the quilt top, the wadding (batting) and the backing. Quilt as desired and bind to finish (see General Techniques: Binding a Quilt).

WAYFARER

The block in this quilt is an easy one to piece, which makes the quilt a good one for a weekend project. It's worth taking a little extra care when squaring up your blocks as you need to allow an extra ¼in seam allowance around the edges of the squares. When sorting colours be guided by what you have in your jelly roll. You could use a colour where we have used neutrals – that's what makes our quilts all individual. The Moda jelly roll we used, The Wordsmith by Janet Clare, worked brilliantly.

VITAL STATISTICS

Finished size: 55in square

Block size: 11¼in square (finished)

Number of blocks: 16

Setting: 4 x 4, plus sashing 2in wide (finished)

YOU WILL NEED

- One jelly roll (or forty 2½in x width of fabric strips from your stash)

- Long ¼yd (25cm) of neutral fabric to coordinate with jelly roll, cut into three 2½in wide strips

- 1⅛yds (1m) of sashing fabric

- ½yd (50cm) of binding fabric

PREPARATION AND CUTTING

SORTING THE STRIPS

Sort your strips into the following groups – artistic licence can be used here but don't stray too far as you may lose the design.

- Fourteen neutral strips, plus three strips cut from the extra-long ¼yd (seventeen strips in total).
- Twelve grey strips.
- Eight blue strips.
- Four green strips.
- Two strips for sashing squares (green or whatever colour is left).

CUTTING THE NEUTRAL JELLY ROLL STRIPS

Take two strips and cut each into sixteen 2½in squares to make a total of thirty-two 2½in neutral squares. Leave the remaining fifteen strips uncut.

CUTTING THE JELLY ROLL STRIPS FOR SASHING SQUARES

Cut each of the two strips allocated for the sashing squares into sixteen 2½in squares. You will need twenty-five squares.

CUTTING THE SASHING FABRIC

Cut fourteen 2½in wide strips across the width of the fabric. Do not sub-cut these strips until you have measured the size of your finished block after trimming. Our block measured 11¾in x 11¾in, so we then sub-cut each strip into three rectangles 2½in x 11¾in to make a total of forty-two sashing strips. You need forty, so two are spare. Note: If your seams are a little wider or narrower, your block will measure a little more or a little

less. Cut your sashing strips to this measurement: they must, of course, all be the same.

CUTTING THE BINDING FABRIC

Cut six 2½in wide strips across the width of fabric.

MAKING THE QUILT

SEWING THE STRIP UNITS

1 Sew the following strip units, as shown in the diagram. When sewing strips together, sew one strip in place, sewing in one direction, and add the next strip by sewing in the opposite direction, and so on. This will prevent the strip unit 'bowing'. Press the seams in the directions shown by the arrows.

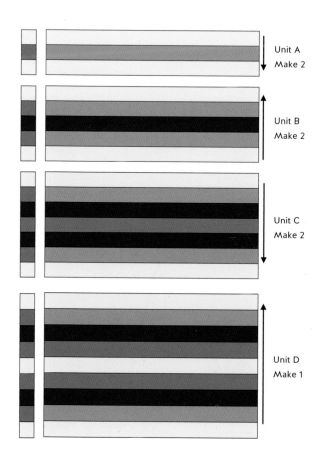

Unit A
Make 2

Unit B
Make 2

Unit C
Make 2

Unit D
Make 1

TIP: YOU NEED TO CHANGE (OR SHARPEN) YOUR ROTARY CUTTER BLADE AS SOON AS IT GETS BLUNT TO GET THE BEST FROM YOUR ROTARY CUTTING EQUIPMENT.

The quilt was made by the authors and long-arm quilted by The Quilt Room.

2 Cut each strip unit into sixteen 2½in segments. Keep the units in separate piles.

4 Repeat this process to make sixteen blocks in total, pressing each sewn block well.

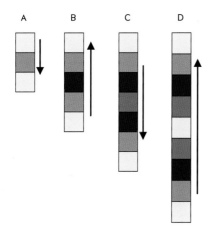

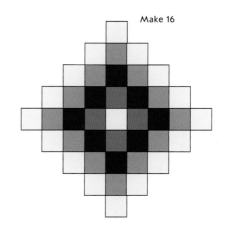

Make 16

ASSEMBLING THE BLOCKS

3 For one block, take two segments from strip units A, B and C, one segment from strip unit D and two 2½in neutral squares. Sew the units together to form one block, in the arrangement shown in the diagram, pinning at every seam intersection to ensure a perfect match. Press the seams in the directions indicated by the arrows.

5 Trim each block by rotating a block and, using a large quilting square, square up the block to measure 11¾in, making sure that you allow ¼in seam allowance around the outside of the squares. The outside of your block now has bias edges, which need to be treated gently. Note: If your seams have been sewn slightly wider or narrower, then your measurement will vary slightly.

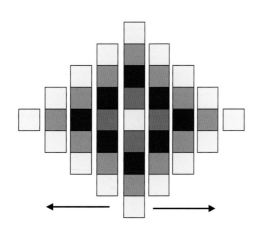

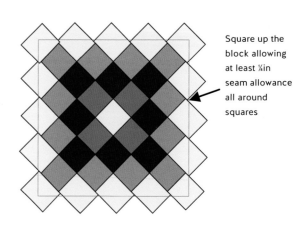

Square up the block allowing at least ¼in seam allowance all around squares

ASSEMBLING THE QUILT

6 Now cut your sashing strips to the exact measurement of your block. Sew four sashing strips together with five sashing squares, as shown. Press towards the sashing strips. Repeat to make five units.

Make 5

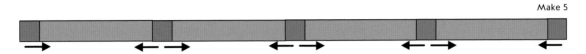

7 Sew four blocks together in a row with sashing strips on both sides of the first block and on the right-hand side of the other three blocks, as shown. Press towards the sashing strips. Repeat to make four rows.

8 Sew all rows together, pinning at seam intersections to ensure a perfect match. Press the seams. Your quilt top is now complete.

QUILTING AND FINISHING

9 Make a quilt sandwich of the quilt top, the wadding (batting) and the backing. Quilt as desired and then bind to finish (see General Techniques: Binding a Quilt).

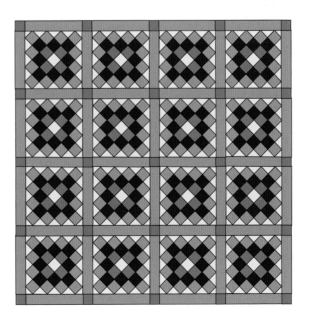

HONEYCOMB

Hexagons are always fun and the strippy ones in this quilt are quick to make as they are pieced half-hexagons sewn together, with no set-in seams needed. You need to use a jelly roll that has a range of colours, as the design would be lost if you had hexagons of similar colours next to each other. We used a lovely jelly roll from Blackbird Designs called Wild Orchid. We loved the range of pinks, lilacs and yellows going deeper into browns and blacks. It was the perfect choice for this quilt. We edged it with a solid taupe border, which sets the fabrics off nicely.

VITAL STATISTICS

Finished size: 55in x 65in

YOU WILL NEED

- One jelly roll (or forty 2½in x width of fabric strips from your stash)

- 1½yds (1.4m) of border fabric

- ½yd (50cm) of binding fabric

- Creative Grids 60-degree triangle measuring at least 8in (or similar triangle)

PREPARATION AND CUTTING

SORTING THE JELLY ROLL STRIPS

Pair up the forty jelly roll strips into twenty pairs. Try to have each fabric in a pair in a similar colour, although if you have duplicates in your jelly roll avoid using them together, as you will lose the strippy effect.

CUTTING THE BORDER FABRIC

- Cut seven 4½in strips across the width of the fabric (for half-hexagons).
- Cut three 5in strips across the width of the fabric (for top and bottom borders).

CUTTING THE BINDING FABRIC

Cut six 2½in wide strips across the width of the fabric.

TIP: WE MANAGED TO CUT SIX HALF-HEXAGONS FROM SOME OF OUR LONGER STRIPS AND ALTHOUGH YOU DO NOT NEED EXTRA, IT DOES GIVE YOU A LITTLE MORE CHOICE WHEN LAYING OUT THE HEXAGONS PRIOR TO SEWING.

MAKING THE QUILT

STRIP PIECING THE HEXAGONS

1 Sew your pairs of jelly roll strips into twenty strip units. Press in the direction shown by the arrow in the diagram.

Make 20

2 Take one of these strip units and place the 60-degree triangle on the strip as shown in the diagram, with the 3½in line of the ruler along the top and the 8in line along the bottom. Mark these lines on the triangle with masking tape to make sure you always line up on the correct markings. Cut the first half-hexagon.

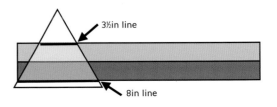

3 Rotate the triangle 180 degrees and continue in this way to cut five half-hexagons from one strip unit (see Tip).

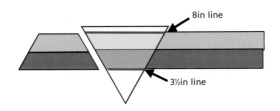

The quilt was made by the authors and long-arm quilted by The Quilt Room.

4 Repeat with all twenty strip units to cut at least 100 jelly roll half-hexagons. Keep the half-hexagons from each strip unit together.

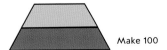

Make 100

6 Repeat with all seven 4½in border strips to make a total of thirty-five border half-hexagons. You need thirty-four, so one will be spare.

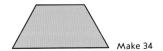

Make 34

5 Take a 4½in border strip and using the same marked triangle, cut five border half-hexagons from one strip, rotating the ruler 180 degrees alternately along the strip.

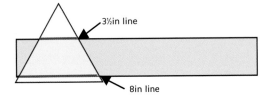

3½in line

8in line

ASSEMBLING THE QUILT

7 Lay out the pieced half-hexagons to form full hexagons as shown in the diagram, trying not to have similar colours next to each other. Place the border half-hexagons at the end of each row and insert as shown in the top and bottom rows. You will have some half-hexagons spare.

8 When you are happy with the layout, sew the half-hexagons into rows. When joining strips with angled cuts there will be an overlap at each end, as shown in the diagram, so check for accuracy.

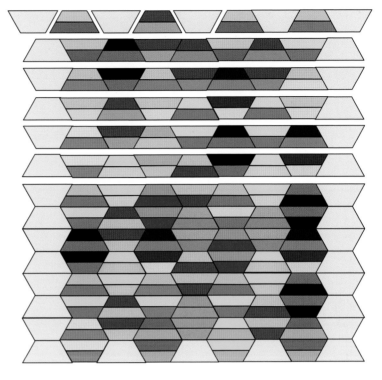

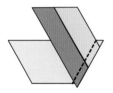

9 When you have finished the first row, press the seams in one direction. Continue sewing rows, pressing the seams of alternate rows in opposite directions so that when sewing the rows together the seams will nest together nicely.

10 Sew the rows together, pinning at all seam intersections to ensure a perfect match, and then press.

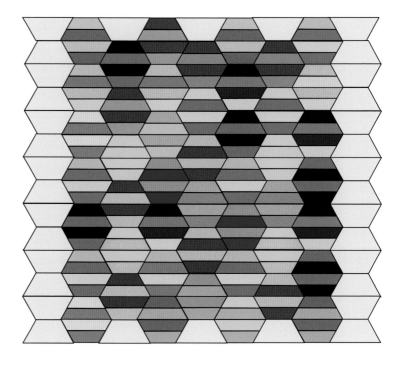

11 Using a long quilting ruler, straighten the uneven side edges of the quilt.

TIP: DO LABEL YOUR QUILTS ON THE BACK BECAUSE THE NEXT GENERATION WILL BE INTERESTED TO KNOW WHO MADE A QUILT AND ANY OTHER INTERESTING DETAILS YOU MIGHT ADD. WE LOVE DISCOVERING QUILT LABELS ON ANTIQUE QUILTS. DON'T FORGET TO TAKE PHOTOS!

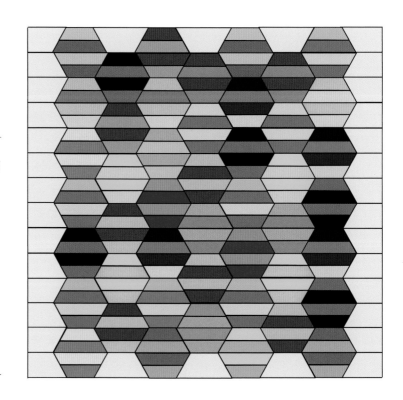

ADDING THE TOP AND BOTTOM BORDERS

12 Sew the three 5in wide border strips into a continuous length. Determine the horizontal measurement of the quilt and cut two borders to this length. Pin and sew to the top and bottom of the quilt and press. Your quilt top is now complete.

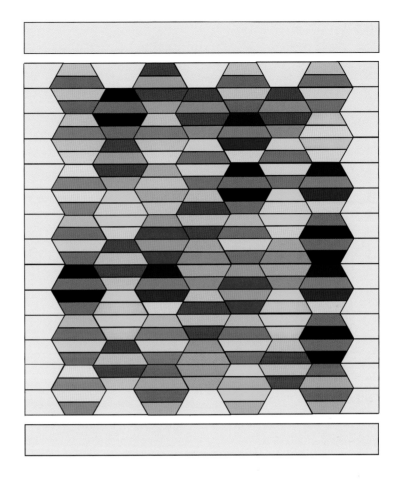

QUILTING AND FINISHING

13 Make a quilt sandwich of the quilt top, the wadding (batting) and the backing. Quilt as desired and bind to finish (see General Techniques: Binding a Quilt).

TUTTI-FRUTTI

This is a great quilt to make if you want to use up any odd jelly roll strips you may have. We decided to use up lots of spare strips we had and as long as the strip was bright and colourful it made its way into our jelly roll. We loved the bright, cheery effect and this quilt is definitely one to make if you need to do a bit of 'stash busting'. The blocks each have two four-patch units, which are strip pieced for speed – chain piecing makes the process even faster. The four-patch units coupled with snowball units create interesting secondary patterns.

VITAL STATISTICS

Finished size: 48in x 64in

Block size: 16in square (finished)

Number of blocks: 12

Setting: 3 x 4 blocks

YOU WILL NEED

- One jelly roll (or forty 2½in x width of fabric strips from your stash)

- 1½yds (1.4m) of pale background fabric

- ½yd (50cm) of binding fabric

PREPARATION AND CUTTING

SORTING THE JELLY ROLL STRIPS

Select the following jelly roll strips (four strips will be spare).

- Twenty-four strips for the four-patch units.
- Twelve strips for the corners of the snowball units.

CUTTING THE JELLY ROLL STRIPS

- Take the twelve strips allocated for the corners of the snowball units and sub-cut each strip into sixteen 2½in squares to make 192 in total.
- Leave the twenty-four strips for the four-patch units uncut.

CUTTING THE BACKGROUND FABRIC

Cut eleven 4½in strips across the width of the fabric. Sub-cut each strip into nine 4½in squares. You will need ninety-six, so three are spare.

CUTTING THE BINDING FABRIC

Cut six 2½in wide strips across the width of the fabric.

TIP: TO MAKE CUTTING FASTER YOU CAN LAYER UP STRIPS BEFORE CUTTING, BUT MAKE SURE YOU DON'T CUT THROUGH TOO MANY AT ONCE OR YOU WILL LOSE ACCURACY.

MAKING THE QUILT

MAKING THE FOUR-PATCH UNITS

1 Choose two contrasting jelly roll strips and lay them right sides together. Sew down the long side. Open and press towards the darker fabric. Repeat with all twenty-four strips allocated for the four-patch units to make a total of twelve strip units, chain piecing for speed.

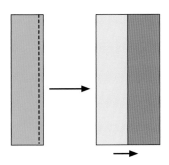

2 Choose two strip units and with right sides together, lay one strip unit on top of another, with the light strip on the top of one unit and on the bottom of another, ensuring that the centre seams are in alignment.

3 Sub-cut into sixteen 2½in wide segments, as shown.

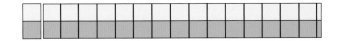

4 Carefully keeping the pairs together, sew down the long side as shown, pinning at the seam intersection to ensure a perfect match. The seams will nest together nicely as they are pressed in different directions. Chain piece for speed. Press open to form sixteen four-patch units.

5 Repeat this process with the remaining strip units to make a total of ninety-six four-patch units.

Make 96

TIP: PRESSING SEAMS IN OPPOSITE DIRECTIONS MAKES IT MUCH EASIER TO MATCH SEAMS NEATLY.

MAKING THE SNOWBALL UNITS

6 Draw a diagonal line from corner to corner on the wrong side of a 2½in square allocated for the snowball unit corners.

7 With right sides together, lay a marked square on one corner of a 4½in background square, aligning the outer edges. Sew across the diagonal, using the marked diagonal line as the stitching line. After a while you may find that you do not need to draw the line as it is not difficult to judge the sewing line. Alternatively, mark the line with a fold.

8 Flip the square over and press towards the outside of the block. Trim the excess fabric from the snowball corner but do not trim the background fabric. Although this creates a little more bulk, the background fabric will help keep your patchwork in shape.

9 Repeat this to sew a square on the opposite corner. Repeat the process to make ninety-six snowball units in total. These can be as scrappy as you like.

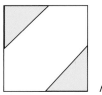

Make 96

The quilt was made by the authors and long-arm quilted by The Quilt Room.

ASSEMBLING A BLOCK

10 Sew a four-patch unit to a snowball unit as shown. Press towards the snowball unit. Repeat with another four-patch unit and a snowball unit. Rotate one sewn unit 180 degrees and sew the two units together to form one quarter-block. Pin at every seam intersection to ensure a perfect match.

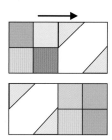

11 Repeat with all ninety-six four-patch units and ninety-six snowball units to create forty-eight quarter-blocks.

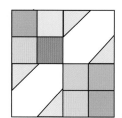

Make 48

12 Sew four quarter-blocks together, rotating two of the quarter-blocks 90 degrees to achieve the pattern shown in the diagram.

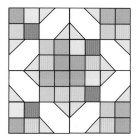

13 Repeat with all forty-eight quarter-blocks to make twelve blocks.

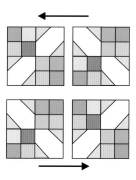

Make 12

14 Lay out the blocks three across and four down as shown. When you are happy with the arrangement sew the blocks into rows and then sew the rows together, pinning at every seam intersection to ensure a perfect match. Your quilt top is now complete.

QUILTING AND FINISHING

15 Make a quilt sandwich of the quilt top, the wadding (batting) and the backing. Quilt as desired and bind to finish (see General Techniques: Binding a Quilt).

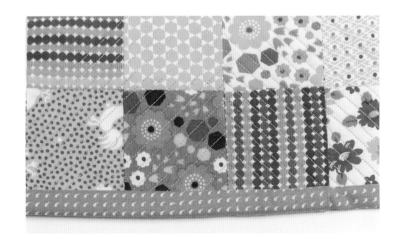

NINE-PATCH SUNBURST

If you are keen enough to want to make lots of nine-patch blocks and then cut them in half then this is the quilt for you! It's actually a fun quilt to make and the piecing can be achieved in a weekend thanks to a strip piecing technique for creating the nine-patch units. It makes a good size quilt with an eye-catching pattern that radiates outwards from the quilt centre. We chose a pastel Kaffe Fassett strip roll and used a Kaffe Fassett pale lilac spot that we really loved for the background, which makes the colours sing.

VITAL STATISTICS

Finished size: 66in square approx

Block size: 5½in square (finished)

Setting: 12 x 12 blocks

YOU WILL NEED

- One jelly roll (or forty 2½in x width of fabric strips from your stash)

- 2¾yds (2.5m) of background fabric

- ½yd (50cm) of binding fabric

PREPARATION AND CUTTING

SORTING THE JELLY ROLL STRIPS

There is no sorting of strips necessary as this is a very scrappy quilt. You will only need thirty-six strips, so four are spare.

CUTTING THE BACKGROUND FABRIC

- Cut eleven 6½in wide strips across the width of the fabric and sub-cut each strip into six 6½in squares to make a total of sixty-six 6½in squares. You need sixty-two, so four are spare.

- Cut three 6in wide strips across the width of the fabric and sub-cut each strip into seven 6in squares to make a total of twenty-one 6in squares. You need twenty, so one is spare.

CUTTING THE BINDING FABRIC

Cut seven 2½in strips across the width of the fabric.

TIP: INSTEAD OF STACKING STRIPS TO SPEED UP CUTTING, TRY BUTTING SINGLE STRIPS UP AGAINST EACH OTHER AND CUTTING MORE STRIPS BUT WITH FEWER LAYERS.

MAKING THE QUILT

SEWING THE NINE-PATCH UNITS

1 Choose three jelly roll strips and sew them together down the long sides to form a strip unit, as shown in the diagram. Sew one strip in one direction and one in the other direction and this will prevent the strip units 'bowing'. Press the sewn strips in one direction, as shown. Repeat with the remaining jelly roll strips to make twelve strip units in total.

Make 12

2 Take each strip unit, trim the selvedge and then cut the strip unit into sixteen 2½in segments.

3 Repeat with all twelve strip units to make a total of 192 segments each 2½in wide. You need 186, so six are spare.

Need 186

The quilt was made by the authors and long-arm quilted by The Quilt Room.

4 Choose two segments and sew together as shown. You may need to rotate one segment so the seams nest together nicely. Pin at the seam intersections to ensure a perfect match, although you may find that once the seams are nested together nicely it is not necessary to pin.

5 Choose a third segment and sew together as shown, rotating the segment so that the seams nest together. Press the seams. The sewn nine-patch unit should be 6½in square.

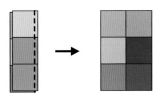

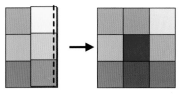

Make 62 nine-patch units

6 Repeat this process to make sixty-two nine-patch units in total. Chain piecing will speed up this process.

ASSEMBLING THE BLOCKS

7 Take the sixty-two 6½in background squares and draw a diagonal line on the reverse side as shown.

10 Press the stitches to set them and then cut along the drawn diagonal line. Trim off dog ears.

11 Open the blocks and press towards the background fabric. Check the block is 6in square at this stage. Repeat with all sixty-two nine-patch units to make 124 blocks in total.

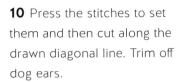

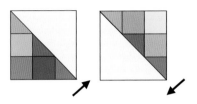

8 Lay one marked background square on top of one nine-patch unit, right sides together and aligning the edges. Pin in position.

9 Stitch along both sides of the drawn line with a scant ¼in seam allowance.

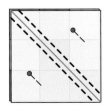

ASSEMBLING THE QUILT

12 Lay out the pieced blocks and the 6in background squares in twelve rows each with twelve blocks, referring to the piecing diagram. Take great care to follow the diagram as it is easy to rotate a block wrongly and spoil the sunburst pattern.

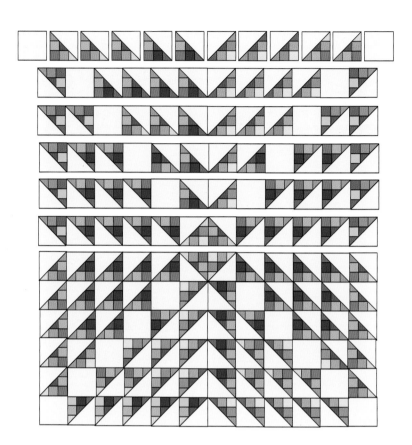

13 When you are happy with the layout sew the blocks into rows and then sew the rows together, pinning at all seam intersections to ensure a perfect match. Your quilt top is now complete.

QUILTING AND FINISHING

14 Make a quilt sandwich of the quilt top, the wadding (batting) and the backing. Quilt as desired and then bind to finish (see General Techniques: Binding a Quilt).

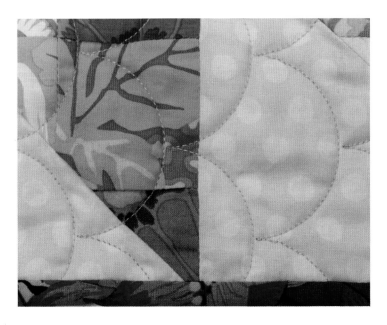

SPROCKETS

The Rolling Stone block has always been a favourite of ours, alternated with other blocks or fabulously alone as in this quilt. This quilt is more of a long weekend project but we felt it justified having a place in the book as it really does piece together well and hey… we just liked it! There are lots of half-square triangle units to make and lots of seams to match but sometimes a challenge is good for us! We used a jelly roll from Moda called Chic Neutrals by Amy Ellis, with a white-on-white background fabric and a black-on-black border.

VITAL STATISTICS

Finished size: 54in square

Block size: 12in square (finished)

Number of blocks: 16

Setting: 4 x 4 blocks, plus 3in border (finished)

YOU WILL NEED

- One jelly roll (or forty 2½in x width of fabric strips from your stash)

- ⅝yd (60cm) of light background fabric

- ½yd (50cm) of dark border fabric

- ½yd (50cm) of binding fabric

- Creative Grids Multi-Size 45/90 ruler for making half-square triangles (or similar ruler)

PREPARATION AND CUTTING

SORTING THE JELLY ROLL STRIPS

Each block is made up of one and a half strips of Colour A, one strip of Colour B and a half-strip of pale background fabric. All of the full strips need to be used as half-strips (2½in x 21in) so it is easier to cut them all into half-strips now, which also helps with the sorting. Try to have the extra half-strip of Colour A as near as possible to the full strip of Colour A. Keep (pin) the three half-strips of Colour A and the strip of Colour B (now cut into two half-strips) together for each of the sixteen blocks. You can add the half-strip of background fabric once cut.

TIP: THE SORTING OF THE FABRICS TAKES A LITTLE TIME. IF YOU COULD DO THIS BEFORE YOUR SEWING WEEKEND IT WOULD SAVE TIME TO HAVE THE STRIPS PINNED TOGETHER, READY TO USE.

CUTTING THE LIGHT BACKGROUND FABRIC

Cut eight 2½in strips across the width of the fabric and then sub-cut each strip in half to make sixteen half-strips 2½in x 21in. One background half-strip is used in each block.

CUTTING THE DARK BORDER FABRIC

Cut five 3½in strips across the fabric width.

CUTTING THE BINDING FABRIC

Cut six 2½in strips across the fabric width.

MAKING THE QUILT

MAKING THE SQUARE UNITS

1 Working with a set of strips for one block at a time, take the colour A half-strip (which is half of the full strip) and one colour B half-strip and sew together as shown. This strip unit should measure 4½in. Press towards colour A, as shown by the arrow in the diagram.

2 Cut the strip unit into four 4½in squares, as shown in the diagram.

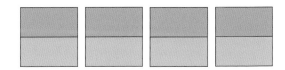

MAKING THE HALF-SQUARE TRIANGLE UNITS

3 Take the remaining half of the full colour A strip used in step 1 and a 2½in wide background half-strip and lay them right sides together on a cutting mat, ensuring that they are exactly one on top of the other.

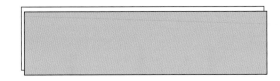

4 Position the Multi-Size 45/90 ruler as shown in the diagram, lining up the 2in mark at the bottom edge of the strips. Trim the selvedge and cut the first pair of triangles. The cut out triangle has a flat top. This would just have been a dog ear you needed to cut off, so it is saving you time.

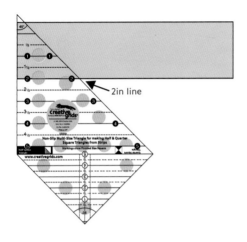

2in line

5 Rotate the ruler 180 degrees as shown and cut the next pair of triangles. Continue along the strip in this way to cut twelve pairs of triangles.

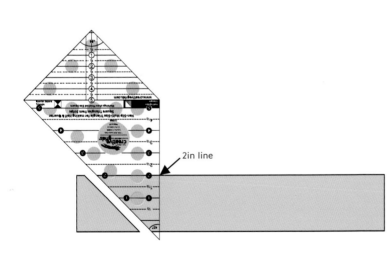

2in line

6 Sew along the diagonal of each pair of triangles. Trim the dog ears and then press eight of the units towards colour A and four of the units towards the background fabric.

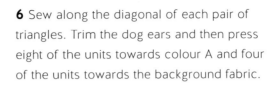

Make 12

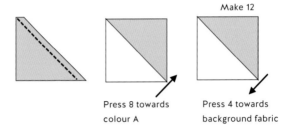

Press 8 towards colour A

Press 4 towards background fabric

7 Take the remaining colour A half-strip and the remaining colour B half-strip and using the ruler as described previously, make four half-square triangles. Press towards the colour B fabric. Set the balance of the strips aside to make the centres of the blocks later.

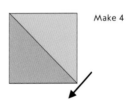

Make 4

8 Sew the half-square triangle units together as shown, making sure you place the colour B fabric in the correct position. Press in the directions shown in the diagram.

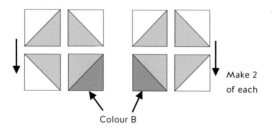

Colour B

Make 2 of each

TIP: IF YOU PUT THE EIGHT UNITS PRESSED TOWARDS COLOUR A IN ONE PILE AND THE EIGHT UNITS PRESSED TOWARDS THE BACKGROUND AND COLOUR B IN ANOTHER, YOU CAN PICK ONE FROM EACH PILE WHEN SEWING THEM TOGETHER. THE SEAMS WILL THEN BE IN OPPOSITE DIRECTIONS AND WILL NEST TOGETHER NICELY.

---

9 Pin the units together, ready to assemble the block once the centres are made. Repeat with all sixteen blocks.

MAKING THE BLOCK CENTRES

10 Choose sixteen of the offcuts you reserved for the centres of the blocks in step 7. Cut each offcut into four 2½in squares and sew them together to make sixteen 4½in centre squares. Remaining offcuts are spare.

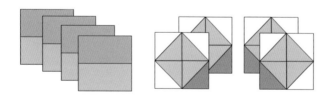

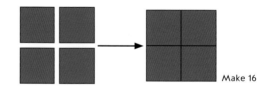

Make 16

ASSEMBLING THE QUILT

11 Working on one block at a time and, referring to the diagram, sew the units together into rows as shown and then sew the rows together. Pin at all seam intersections to ensure a perfect match. Press the seams in the directions shown.

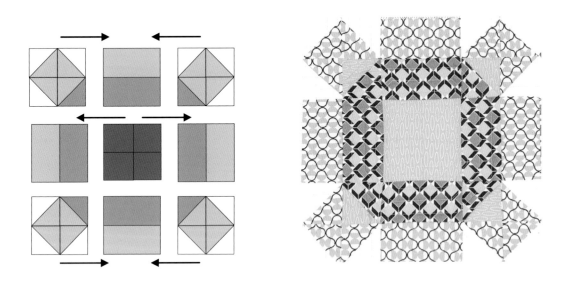

12 Repeat this process to make sixteen blocks in total.

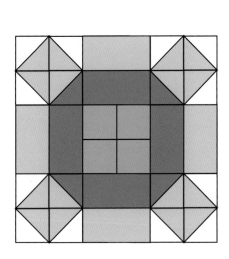

13 Lay out your blocks into four rows of four blocks each. Sew the blocks into rows, pressing the seams of rows 1 and 3 in the opposite direction to rows 2 and 4. Sew the rows together, pinning at all seam intersections to ensure a perfect match.

ADDING THE BORDER

14 Sew the five border strips together end to end. Press the seams open.

15 Determine the vertical measurement from top to bottom through the quilt centre. Cut two side borders to this measurement. Pin and sew to the quilt, easing if necessary.

16 Determine the horizontal measurement from side to side across the quilt centre, including the borders just added. Cut two border strips to this measurement. Pin and sew to the top and bottom of the quilt. Press towards the border. Your quilt top is now complete.

QUILTING AND FINISHING

17 Make a quilt sandwich of the quilt top, the wadding (batting) and the backing. Quilt as desired and then bind to finish (see General Techniques: Binding a Quilt).

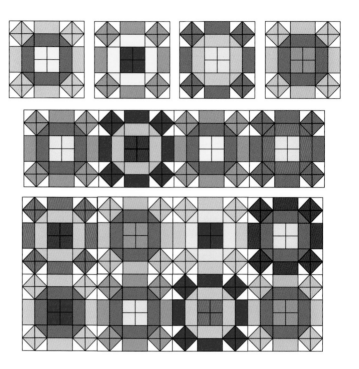

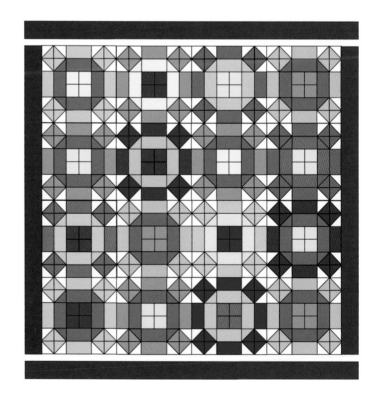

The quilt was made by the authors and long-arm quilted by The Quilt Room.

CIRCLE OF FRIENDS

This quilt uses only half a jelly roll plus background fabric but we have put it at the end of the book because it does take a little longer to make. This is not because it is difficult but because each star block has to be laid out before sewing to ensure that the units are put in the right place – definitely a check twice, sew once block! We have used an antique reproduction range designed by Di Ford-Hall, which creates a lovely mellow look to the quilt.

VITAL STATISTICS

Finished size: 54in square

Block size: 18in square (finished)

Number of blocks: 9

Setting: 3 x 3 blocks

YOU WILL NEED

- Half a jelly roll (or twenty 2½in x width of fabric strips from your stash)

- 2½yds (2.4m) of background fabric

- ½yd (50cm) of binding fabric

- Creative Grids Multi-Size 45/90 ruler for making half-square triangles (or similar ruler)

PREPARATION AND CUTTING

SORTING THE JELLY ROLL STRIPS

- Choose twelve strips to make the half-square triangle units for the Friendship Star blocks and divide these strips into three sets of four strips each. Each set will make three blocks.

- Choose five strips for the centres of the Friendship Stars. Three strips are spare.

CUTTING THE JELLY ROLL STRIPS

- Leave the twelve strips allocated to make half-square triangle units for the Friendship Stars uncut.

- Take the five strips allocated for the centres of the Friendship Stars and cut each into two half-strips 2½in x 21in. You need nine so one half is spare. Cut each half-strip into eight 2½in squares. Keep the eight squares together as they are used together in each of the nine blocks.

CUTTING THE BACKGROUND FABRIC

- Cut two 6½in strips across the width of the fabric and sub-cut into nine 6½in squares.

- Cut thirty 2½in strips across the width of the fabric and sub-cut as follows.

  - Set twelve aside to make half-square triangle units.

  - Sub-cut nine strips into thirty-six 2½in x 8½in rectangles.

  - Sub-cut four strips into thirty-six 2½in x 4½in rectangles.

  - Sub-cut five strips into seventy-two 2½in squares.

CUTTING THE BINDING FABRIC

Cut six 2½in wide strips across the width of the fabric.

MAKING THE QUILT

MAKING THE HALF-SQUARE TRIANGLE UNITS

1 Working with one set of four jelly roll strips at a time, take a jelly roll strip and a 2½in background strip and lay them right sides together ensuring that they are exactly one on top of the other.

2 Position the Multi-Size 45/90 ruler as shown in the diagram, lining up the 2in mark at the bottom edge of the strips. Trim the selvedge and cut the first pair of triangles. The cut out triangle has a flat top. This would just have been a dog ear you needed to cut off, so it is saving you time.

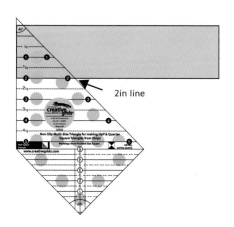

2in line

3 Rotate the ruler 180 degrees as shown and cut the next pair of triangles. Continue like this along the strip, cutting twenty-four pairs of triangles.

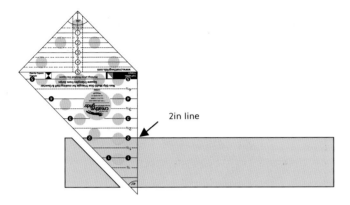

2in line

4 Sew along the diagonal of each pair of triangles. Trim dog's ears and press open towards the jelly roll fabric. Repeat to form twenty-four half-square triangle units.

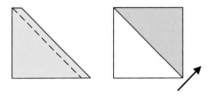

5 Repeat with the remaining three jelly roll strips from the set to make twenty-four half-square triangle units from each. These will make three blocks.

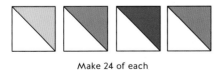

Make 24 of each

ASSEMBLING A BLOCK

6 Working with eight half-square triangle units from each colour and eight centre squares, sew the units into rows with the background squares and rectangles. Refer to the block piecing diagram to ensure that you are sewing the units together correctly. Press in the directions shown by the arrows in the diagram. Refer to steps 7 and 8 below for details of sewing the block.

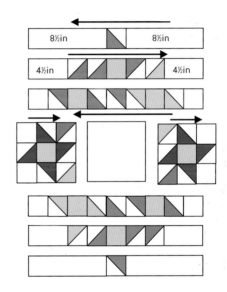

7 Sew the top three rows together first, pinning at each intersection to ensure a perfect match. Press as shown. Repeat to make two of these as they can be rotated 180 degrees to form the bottom three rows.

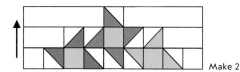

Make 2

8 Sew the left and the right centre sections and sew these to the 6½in centre background square. Double check before sewing that you are using the correct colour and that it is positioned the right way round. It is best to check twice and sew once!

MAKING THE REMAINING BLOCKS

9 Repeat the process with the other two sets of jelly roll strips to make a total of nine blocks. You will find that there are occasions when you have to re-press seams so they nest together nicely.

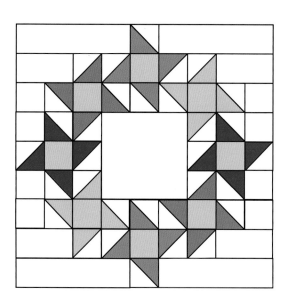

ASSEMBLING THE QUILT

10 Sew the blocks into three rows of three blocks, pinning at all seam intersections. Press the seams of row 2 in the opposite direction to rows 1 and 3. Your quilt is now complete.

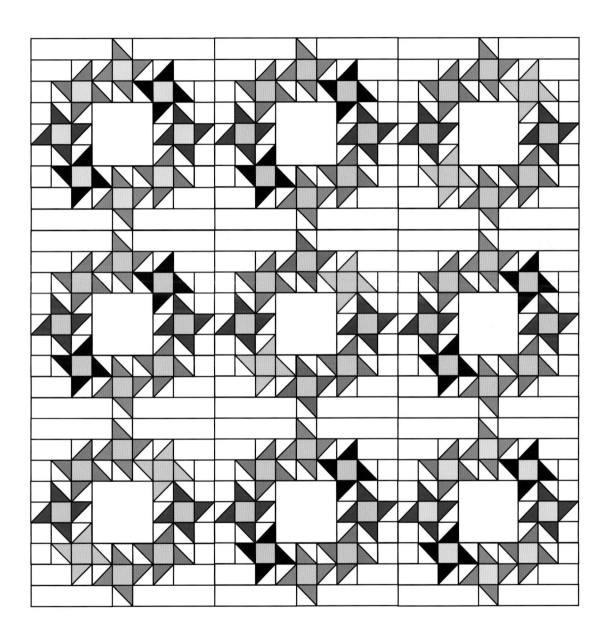

QUILTING AND FINISHING

11 Make a quilt sandwich of the quilt top, the wadding (batting) and the backing. Quilt as desired and bind to finish (see General Techniques: Binding a Quilt).

TIP: ONLY USING HALF A JELLY ROLL GIVES YOU SOME OPTIONS. FOR EXAMPLE, YOU COULD ALSO USE SOME OF THE SPARE STRIPS TO CREATE A SCRAPPY BINDING. OR YOU COULD USE THE WHOLE JELLY ROLL AND MAKE A QUILT DOUBLE THE SIZE. THIS WOULD MAKE EIGHTEEN BLOCKS SO YOUR QUILT WOULD MEASURE 72IN SQUARE AND YOU WOULD ALSO HAVE TWO BLOCKS SPARE FOR MATCHING CUSHIONS. ALTERNATIVELY, YOU COULD SHARE THE JELLY ROLL WITH A FRIEND AND BOTH MAKE A QUILT USING THE SAME JELLY ROLL.

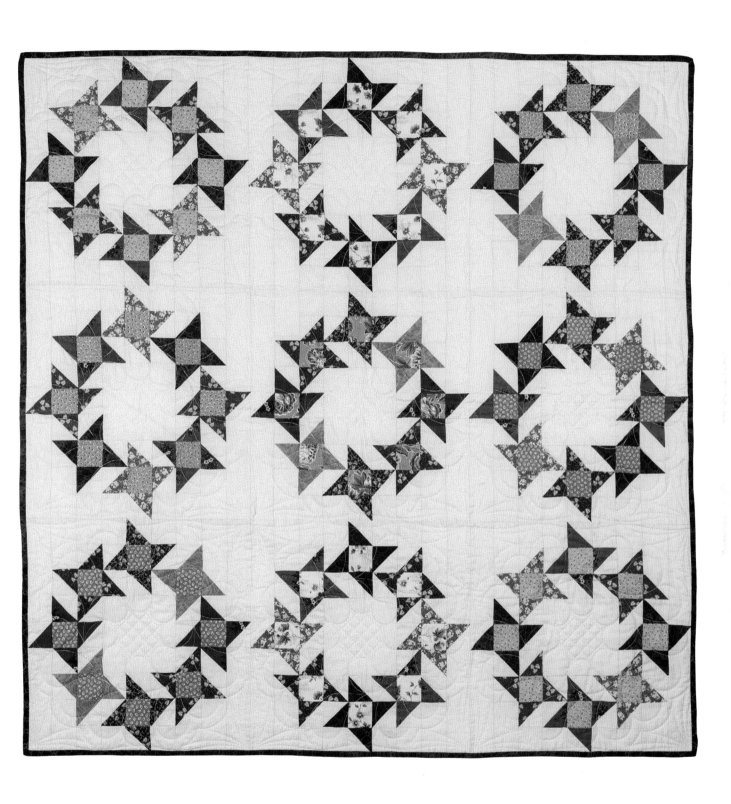

The quilt was made by the authors and long-arm quilted by The Quilt Room.

General Techniques

TOOLS

All the projects in this book require rotary cutting equipment. You will need a self-healing cutting mat at least 18in x 24in and a rotary cutter – 45mm or 60mm diameter. We recommend the 6½in x 24½in ruler as a basic ruler, plus a large square that is handy for squaring up and making sure you are always cutting at right angles. We used a 12½in square in the Wayfarer quilt. We have tried not to use too many speciality rulers but when working with 2½in wide strips you do have to re-think some cutting procedures. You will need a speciality ruler to cut half-square triangles, which is used in Sprockets and Circle of Friends. Creative Grids have designed the Multi-Size 45/90 ruler for us, which is perfect. This ruler shows the finished size measurements. This means that when you are cutting half-square triangles from 2½in strips you line up the 2in marking along the bottom of the strip. This 2in marking relates to the fact that the finished half-square triangle unit will be 2in. If you are using a different ruler, please make sure you are lining up your work on the correct markings.

In our Picnic Time quilt we used a large 60-degree triangle, which can measure up to 12in triangles. This is a great basic ruler to have in your collection.

Items in a basic tool kit could include: a tape measure, rotary cutter, cutting ruler, cutting mat, needles, pins, scissors, fabric marker, iron and sewing machine.

SEAMS

We cannot stress enough the importance of maintaining an accurate ¼in seam allowance throughout. We prefer to say an accurate *scant* ¼in seam because there are two factors to take into account. Firstly, the thickness of thread and secondly, when the seam allowance is pressed to one side it takes up a tiny amount of fabric. These are both extremely small amounts but if they are ignored you will find your exact ¼in seam allowance is taking up more than ¼in. So, it is well worth testing your seam allowance before starting on a quilt. Most sewing machines have various needle positions that can be used to make adjustments.

SEAM ALLOWANCE TEST

To check your seam allowance, take a 2½in strip and cut off three segments each 1½in wide. Sew two segments together down the longer side and press the seam to one side. Sew the third segment across the top. It should fit exactly. If it doesn't, you need to make an adjustment to your seam allowance. If it is too long, your seam allowance is too wide and can be corrected by moving the needle on your sewing machine to the right. If it is too small, your seam allowance is too narrow and this can be corrected by moving the needle to the left.

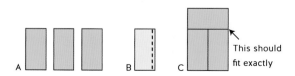

This should fit exactly

PRESSING

In quiltmaking, pressing is important and if care is taken you will be well rewarded. This is especially true when dealing with strips, because if strips start 'bowing' and stretching you will lose accuracy.

- Always set your seam after sewing by pressing the seam as sewn, without opening up your strips. This eases any tension and prevents the seam line from distorting. Move the iron with an up and down motion, zigzagging along the seam rather than ironing down the length of the seam, which could cause distortion.

- Open up your strips and press on the right side of the fabric towards the darker fabric, if necessary guiding the seam underneath to make sure the seam is going in the right direction. Press with an up and down motion rather than along the strip length.

- Always take care if using steam and certainly don't use steam anywhere near a bias edge.

- When you are joining more than two strips together, it is best to press the seams after attaching each strip. You are more likely to get bowing if you leave it until your strip unit is complete before pressing.

- Each seam must be pressed flat before another seam is sewn across it. Unless there is a special reason for not doing so, seams are pressed towards the darker fabric. The main criteria when joining seams, however, is to have the seam allowances going in the opposite direction to each other as they then nest together without bulk. Your patchwork will lie flat and your seam intersections will be accurate.

PINNING

Don't underestimate the benefits of pinning. When you have to align a seam it is important to insert pins to stop any movement when sewing. Long, fine pins with flat heads are recommended as they will go through the layers of fabric easily and allow you to sew up to and over them. Insert a pin either at right angles or diagonally through the seam intersection, ensuring that the seams are matching perfectly. When sewing, do not remove the pin too early as your fabric might shift and the seams will not be perfectly aligned. Seams should always be pressed in opposite directions so they will nest together nicely.

CHAIN PIECING

Chain piecing is the technique of feeding a series of pieces through the sewing machine without lifting the presser foot and without cutting the thread between each piece. Always chain piece when you can as it saves time and thread. Once your chain is complete simply snip the thread between the pieces. When chain piecing shapes other than squares and rectangles it is sometimes preferable when finishing one shape, to lift the presser foot slightly and reposition on the next shape, still leaving the thread uncut.

REMOVING DOG EARS

A dog ear is the excess piece of fabric that overlaps past the seam allowance when sewing triangles to other shapes. Dog ears should always be cut off to reduce bulk. They can be trimmed using a rotary cutter although snipping with small, sharp scissors is quicker. Make sure you are trimming the points parallel to the straight edge of the triangle.

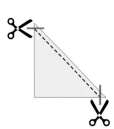

JOINING BORDER AND BINDING STRIPS

If you need to join strips for your borders and binding, you may choose to join them with a diagonal seam to make them less noticeable, although please be aware that such seams will take up more fabric, so check that you have enough. Press the seams open.

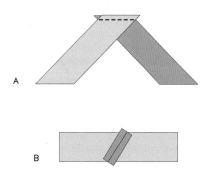

ADDING BORDERS

The fabric requirements in this book all assume you are going to be sewing straight rather than mitred borders. If you intend to have mitred borders please add sufficient extra fabric for this.

ADDING STRAIGHT BORDERS

1 Determine the vertical measurement from top to bottom through the centre of the quilt top. Cut two side border strips to this measurement. Mark the halves and quarters of one quilt side and one border with pins. Placing right sides together and matching the pins, stitch the quilt and border together, easing the quilt side to fit where necessary. Repeat on the opposite side. Press the seams open.

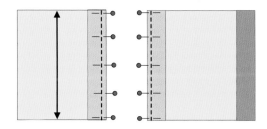

2 Determine the horizontal measurement from side to side across the centre of the quilt top. Cut two top and bottom border strips to this measurement and add to the quilt top in the same manner.

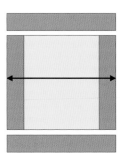

QUILTING

Quilting stitches hold the patchwork top, wadding (batting) and backing together and create texture over your finished patchwork. The choice is yours whether you hand quilt, machine quilt or send it off to a long-arm quilting service. There are many books dedicated to the techniques of hand and machine quilting but the basic procedure is as follows.

1 With the aid of templates or a ruler, mark out the quilting lines on the patchwork top.

2 Cut the backing fabric and wadding (batting) at least 4in larger all around than the patchwork top. Pin or tack (baste) the layers together to prepare them for quilting.

3 Quilt either by hand or by machine. Remove any quilting marks or tacking (basting) on completion of the quilting.

BINDING A QUILT

The fabric requirements given in the book are for a 2½in double-fold binding cut on the straight grain.

1 Trim the excess backing and wadding (batting) so that the edges are even with the top of the quilt.

2 Join the binding strips into a continuous length, making sure there is sufficient to go around the quilt plus 8in–10in for corners and overlapping ends. With wrong sides together, press the binding in half lengthways. Fold and press under ½in to neaten the edge at the end where you will start sewing.

3 On the right side of the quilt and starting about 12in away from a corner, align the raw edges of the double thickness binding with the edge of the quilt, so that the cut edges are towards the edges of the quilt. Pin to hold in place. Sew with a ¼in seam allowance, leaving the first inch or so open.

4 At the first corner, stop ¼in from the edge of the fabric and backstitch (see diagram A). Lift the needle and presser foot and fold the binding upwards (B). Fold the binding again but downwards (C). Stitch from the edge to ¼in from the next corner and repeat the turn.

5 Continue all around the quilt working each corner in the same way. When you come to the starting point, cut the binding, fold under the cut edge and overlap at the starting point.

6 Fold the binding over to the back of the quilt and hand stitch in place, folding the binding at each corner to form a neat mitre.

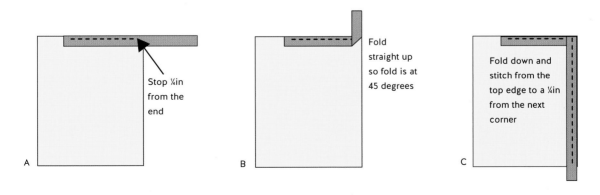

A — Stop ¼in from the end

B — Fold straight up so fold is at 45 degrees

C — Fold down and stitch from the top edge to a ¼in from the next corner

MAKING A LARGER QUILT

If you want to make a larger version of any of the quilts in the book, refer to the Vital Statistics of the quilt, which shows the block size, the number of blocks, how the blocks are set plus the size of border used. You can use this information to re-calculate your requirements for a larger quilt.

SETTING ON POINT

Any block can take on a totally new look when set on point and you might like to try one of the quilts to see what it looks like on point. For this reason we have included information here for setting quilts on point. Some people are a little daunted as there are a few things to take into account but here is all you really need to know.

HOW WIDE WILL MY BLOCKS BE WHEN SET ON POINT?

To calculate the measurement of the block from point to point, multiply the size of the finished block by 1.414. Example: a 12in block will measure 12in x 1.414 which is 16.97in (17in). Now you can calculate how many blocks you need for your quilt.

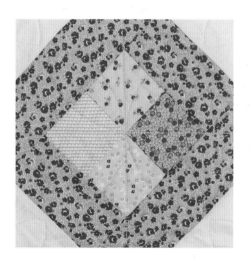

HOW DO I PIECE BLOCKS ON POINT?

Piece rows diagonally, starting at a corner. Triangles have to be added to the end of each row before joining the rows and these are called setting triangles. See Fruit Punch for an example of a quilt set on point.

HOW DO I CALCULATE WHAT SIZE SETTING TRIANGLES TO CUT?

Setting triangles form the outside of your quilt and need to have the straight of grain on the outside edge to prevent stretching. To ensure this, these triangles are formed from quarter-square triangles, i.e., a square cut into four triangles. The measurement for this is: Diagonal Block Size + 1¼in.
Example: a 12in block (diagonal measurement approximately 17in) should be 18¼in.

Corners triangles are added last. They also need to have the outside edge on the straight grain, so these should be cut from half-square triangles. To calculate the size of square to cut in half, divide the finished size of your block by 1.414 then add ⅞in.
Example: a 12in block would be 12in divided by 1.414 = 8.49in + ⅞in (0.88) = 9.37in (or 9½in as it can be trimmed later).

Most diagonal quilts start off with one block and in each row thereafter the number of blocks increase by two. All rows contain an odd number of blocks. To calculate the finished size of the quilt, count the number of diagonals across and multiply this by the diagonal measurement of the block. Do the same with the number of blocks down and multiply this by the diagonal measurement of the block.

If you want a rectangular quilt instead of a square one, count the number of blocks in the row that establishes the width and repeat that number in following rows until the desired length is established.

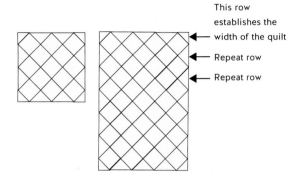

This row establishes the width of the quilt

← Repeat row

← Repeat row

CALCULATING BACKING FABRIC

The patterns in this book do not include fabric requirements for backing as many people like to use extra wide backing fabric so they do not have to have any joins.

USING 60IN WIDE FABRIC

This is a simple calculation as to how much you need to buy. Example: your quilt is 54in x 72in. Your backing needs to be 3in larger all round so your backing measurement needs to be 60in x 78in. If you have found 60in wide backing, then you would buy the length, which is 78in. However, if you have found 90in wide backing, you can turn it round and would only have to buy the width of 60in.

USING 42IN WIDE FABRIC

For this width you will need to have a join or joins to get the required measurement, unless the backing measurement for your quilt is 42in or less on one side. If your backing measurement is less than 42in then you need only buy one length.

Using the previous example, if your backing measurement is 60in x 78in, you will have to have one seam somewhere in your backing. If you join two lengths of 42in fabric together your new fabric measurement will be 84in (less a little for the seam). This would be sufficient for the length of your quilt so you need to buy two times the width, i.e., 60in x 2 = 120in. Your seam will run horizontal.

If your quilt length is more than your new backing fabric measurement of 84in you will need to use the measurement of 84in for the quilt width and will have to buy two times the length. The seam will then run vertically.

LABELLING YOUR QUILT

When you have finished your quilt it is important to label it, even if the information you put on the label is just your name and the date. When looking at antique quilts it is always interesting to see information about the quilt, so you can be sure that any extra information you put on the label will be of immense interest to quilters of the future. For example, you could say when and why you made the quilt and who it was for, or for what special occasion. Labels can be as ornate as you like, but a simple and quick method is to write on a piece of calico with a permanent marker pen and then appliqué this to the back of your quilt.

Useful Contacts

The Quilt Room
37–39 High Street, Dorking,
Surrey, RH4 1AR, UK
Tel: 01306 877307
www.quiltroom.co.uk

Sew and So
Tel: 0800 013 0150
www.sewandso.co.uk

Moda Fabrics/United Notions
13800 Hutton Drive, Dallas,
Texas 75234, USA
Tel: 800-527-9447
www.modafabrics.com

Janome UK Ltd
Janome Centre, Southside,
Stockport, Cheshire,
SK6 2SP, UK
Tel: 0161 666 6011
www.janome.co.uk

Acknowledgments

We would like to thank the team at Moda Fabrics for their continued support and for allowing us to use the name 'jelly roll' in the title and throughout the book. Thanks to Janome Sewing Machines for allowing us the use of their reliable sewing machines when making up the quilts for this book. Thanks to the girls at The Quilt Room who keep The Quilt Room running smoothly when we are rushing to meet tight deadlines. Last, but most definitely not least, our extra special thanks to Pam's husband Nick and to Nicky's husband Rob, for looking after everything that needs to be done when deadlines are being met and computers and sewing machines are working overtime.

About the Authors

Pam Lintott opened her quilt shop, The Quilt Room, in 1981, which she still runs today, along with her daughter Nicky. In 2016 they celebrated thirty-five years from the opening of their shop – the oldest quilt shop in the UK. Pam is the author of *The Quilt Room Patchwork & Quilting Workshops*, as well as *The Quilter's Workbook*.

Jelly Roll Quilts in a Weekend is Pam and Nicky's twelfth book for David & Charles. They remember with a smile their discussions with David & Charles about their first book – the phenomenally successful *Jelly Roll Quilts* – when Pam and Nicky advised speeding up publication as the idea of jelly rolls might not last!

Index

A SEWANDSO BOOK
© F&W Media International, Ltd 2017

SewandSo is an imprint of F&W Media International, Ltd
Pynes Hill Court, Pynes Hill, Exeter, EX2 5AZ

F&W Media International, Ltd is a subsidiary of F+W Media, Inc
10151 Carver Road, Suite #200, Blue Ash, OH 45242, USA

Text and Designs © Pam and Nicky Lintott 2017
Layout and Photography © F&W Media International, Ltd 2017

First published in the UK and USA in 2017

Pam and Nicky Lintott have asserted their right to be identified as authors of this work in accordance with the
Copyright, Designs and Patents Act, 1988.

A catalogue record for this book is available from the British Library.

ISBN-13: 978-1-4463-0657-4 paperback
SRN: R4953 paperback

ISBN-13: 978-1-4463-7505-1 PDF
SRN: R5024 PDF

ISBN-13: 978-1-4463-7504-4 EPUB
SRN: R5025 EPUB

Printed in China by RR Donnelley for:
F&W Media International, Ltd
Pynes Hill Court, Pynes Hill, Exeter, EX2 5AZ

10 9 8 7 6 5 4 3 2 1

Content Manager: Sarah Callard
Senior Editor: Jeni Hennah
Project Editor: Linda Clements
Design Manager: Anna Wade
Production Manager: Beverley Richardson
Design: Lorraine Inglis, Lisa Fordham and Ali Stark
Photography: Jason Jenkins
Art Direction and Styling: Prudence Rogers

F&W Media publishes high quality books on a wide range of subjects.
For more great book ideas visit: www.sewandso.co.uk

Layout of the digital edition of this book may vary depending on reader hardware and display settings.